Beyond the Pride and the Privilege: The Stories of Doctoral Students and Work-Life Balance

A Volume in:
Work-Life Balance

Series Editors
Joanne M. Marshall
Jeffrey S. Brooks
Bonnie Fusarelli
Catherine A. Lugg
Latish C. Reed
George Theoharis

Work-Life Balance

Series Editors

Juggling Flaming Chain Saws: Academics in Educational Leadership Try to Balance Work and Family (2012)
Edited by Joanne M. Marshall, Jeffrey S. Brooks, Kathleen M. Brown, Leslie Hazle Bussey, Bonnie Fusarelli, Mark A. Gooden, Catherine A. Lugg, Latish C. Reed, and George Theoharis

Beyond the Pride and the Privilege: The Stories of Doctoral Students and Work-Life Balance

Edited by

Agustina Veny Purnamasari
B. Genise Henry
Chinasa A. Elue
Edna Martinez

INFORMATION AGE PUBLISHING, INC.
Charlotte, NC • www.infoagepub.com

Library of Congress Cataloging-in-Publication Data

The CIP data for this book can be found on the Library of Congress website (loc.gov).

Paperback: 978-1-62396-906-6
Hardcover: 978-1-62396-907-3
eBook: 978-1-62396-908-0

Book cover design by Donna Le.

Printed in the United States of America

CONTENTS

FOREWORD

Marybeth Gasman

I gave birth to my beautiful daughter Chloe in April 1999 and graduated with my PhD in May 2000. The year leading up to my graduation was strenuous but rewarding. I remember when I told my dissertation committee chair that I was pregnant. His response was, "Why are you telling me this?" In the back of my mind, I knew why. I wanted him to know that although I was going to have a child, I was serious about being an academic. Why did I feel the need to explain my commitment to academe? If I were a man, an explanation would not be necessary and my drive, commitment, or potential success would not be questioned.

Interestingly, the female professors in my circle did not have children so they couldn't offer advice on how I was going to manage being a doctoral student and having a child. I also noticed that many of the women that I met in academe had detached marriages in which they rarely mentioned their partners or led very separate lives. I had no intention of living like that.

I have always been very good at balancing the various aspects of my life. Even before deciding to have a baby, I had worked full-time during part of my PhD program. I learned how to keep my work at work and my academic life at home. I was keenly disciplined and I communicated this discipline with my supervisor at work. When I was at work, I was full on, and rarely wasted any time and when I was at home, I was focused on my coursework. Discipline and focus have been the secrets to my success from the time I was a doctoral student through the cur-

Beyond the Pride and the Privilege: The Stories of Doctoral Students and Work-Life Balance, pages vii–x.

rent day. However, adding a child to the mix made it difficult to be focused and disciplined.

During my pregnancy, I worked full time at an African American community center and was writing my dissertation. There were days that I was simply too exhausted to work on my writing. I felt guilty when I would go to bed early instead of writing a new chapter of my dissertation. However, I knew that I was protecting, growing, and nurturing a new life inside me. I had to come to terms with balance even before my daughter was born. It was at this time that I realized the importance of sleep, exercise, and relaxation to a healthy life—a life that was the incubator for another life. Knowing that you are growing another inside you is a great motivator for taking good care of yourself.

Once my daughter was born, life became more complex and somewhat difficult. I had to ask for help both from my husband and my mother. I knew that I was the kind of person that could not stay at home and be with my child all day. I would go insane without adult interaction and I was willing to admit that. My husband was a tenure track professor and as such, he could only stay home one day a week. I thought it was important to support him in his quest for an academic position. Needing help—and it's important to admit when you do—I asked my mom to make a temporary move to live near me. She had been living with my younger sister. Having her with me the first year of Chloe's life was not only needed, but it was amazing. The three of us—my mom, Chloe and me—formed a bond that continues to this day.

My mom, an uneducated woman who raised 10 children and outlived three husbands, gave me some of the best advice for being a mother and doctoral student even though she had never attended college, let alone earned a PhD. She knew all kinds of strategies for getting things done while also taking care of a child. She had to be organized with ten children. I remember that she told me two really important things—these may sound silly but they helped me finish my dissertation. First, she said, "Don't teach your child to walk. Let her do it on her own. You need all the time you can get before she walks to finish your dissertation." Most parents push their children to achieve new milestones, often before they are ready. I didn't. I listened to my mom and Chloe walked when she was ready. In the meantime, I was able to work on my dissertation while Chloe sat in place playing with her toys and loving her stuffed animals. My mom also told me not to hurry into solid foods. Again, this advice might sound crazy, but it isn't. Babies don't need solid food right away and introducing it takes a lot of time and experimentation. I waited and used my extra time to write my dissertation.

My mom also taught me that babies need alone time and coping skills. She told me not to run to Chloe every time she made a peep—let her console herself. Not only did this advice help me to concentrate when writing my dissertation, but it helped me to sleep at night. By allowing Chloe to learn to lull herself to sleep, I was able to get a full night's sleep as my dear baby slept through the night by 3 months. My mother's experience raising children helped me to have balance while I finished writing my dissertation. All too often we think we know more than our mothers—or parents for that matter—but sometimes we are wrong. Listening to others and accepting their help is a key to balance in one's life.

In the months after Chloe was born, I worked diligently on my dissertation and job search. I learned that when I spent time on my writing in the evenings, I needed to focus. I discussed this need with my husband and he was supportive, taking care of our daughter. I also learned that when I was spending time with Chloe and my family—I needed to be focused on them—and not thinking about my research, writing, or job search. I learned to compartmentalize the various aspects of my life. Occasionally, these compartments would overlap, but I became good at keeping them fairly separate.

As I approached the faculty job search, issues of work and family balance were at the forefront of my mind. I wasn't sure if I should mention having a child during interviews. I asked my mentors and they had varying opinions and told me many horror stories. As a result, I decided to mention that I was married but did not discuss my child. Keep in mind that I was on the job search prior to Facebook so it was very easy to hide having a child from potential employers. It would be nearly impossible for me to do this now. Interestingly, during my interviews, people would try to find out if I had a child by asking round about questions such as "do you need information on the school system?" I typically said, "No." Once I had an offer, I'd let the institution know that I had a child. I do want to note that when I applied for my second faculty job, I was upfront about having a 4 year old. I was more confident and I realized after working in a male-dominated, "hostile toward children" environment, I wanted to be at an institution that valued children. I'm in education dammit—valuing children should be a given.

Balancing being a wife, partner, mother, and graduate student was challenging but it wasn't impossible. It made me organized and strong and led me on my way to being able to balance work and family as a professor, which is much, much harder. My secret to being productive and prolific is to lead a balanced life. This means that I eat regular meals (too many academics eat poorly), I exercise nearly every day in addition to walking to work and around campus during the day (academics spend a lot of time sitting on their rear ends), I socialize with friends about three times a week, and I take vacations. One of the most important things that I do is put my family first above my role as a professor. This doesn't mean that I'm not focused or that I don't take it very seriously—I do—but at the end of the day, my daughter is most important in my life and will always supersede the writing of an article. You only have one chance with your children; there are always revise and resubmits and other opportunities to write articles. However, that's not an excuse to slack off in your writing responsibilities—you just have to be disciplined, fierce and vigilant in your pursuit of your scholarship and in your pursuit of work/family balance.

The last secret that I have beyond balance is saying "no" to opportunities and requests that are not central to your academic career. As you move through the tenure track, many things will be asked of you and myriad opportunities will be placed in front of you. You have to focus—only participate in the things that are connected to your specific interests. Learn to say no gracefully and with a lovely smile. It is a delicate and important skill that will help you achieve the balance you are looking for in life.

I told you my story as a way of introducing this beautiful book of stories, written by graduate students striving to achieve work-life balance—sometimes succeeding and sometimes failing in their pursuit. This is the kind of book that would have been valuable to me as I worked my way through figuring out how to balance the various aspects of my life. Beyond the Pride and the Privilege: The Stories of Doctoral Students and Work-Life Balance is a vivid portrayal of the diverse lives and juggling acts of doctoral students, striving to be good academics, partners, parents, friends, children and people in the midst of the pressure cooker of academe. Not only is it an essential read for current doctoral students and potential doctoral students, but faculty and academic administrators should read it and factor in the complex and full lives of doctoral students at their universities and those that they hire for faculty positions. Most highly successful companies have realized that having a healthy work-life balance leads to better ideas and more productivity—providing childcare, gyms, yoga classes, healthy food choices to their employees as part of their compensation. When will academe catch up and realize that work-life balance will lead to deeper intellectual thought, more innovative ideas, and more committed and caring teaching of our youth? Perhaps this book can serve as a starting point.

INTRODUCTION

Suitably, as the image of the burned out faculty member has become all too familiar, the topic of work life balance has become increasingly common in the higher education literature. As the next generation of faculty is inescapably impacted by the conditions and demands faced by their supervising faculty, the topic of balance is equally important for doctoral students.

More often than not, we forget that our lives consist of much more than research, conferences, and publications; we forget that our family and friends need to be included in our busy schedules. If you find yourself saying, "I don't have time for that; I have too much work to do," chances are that those are the times when you are working 'too much' as opposed to having too much work to do. How often have you made a commitment to write a proposal for a project, agreed to serve on a student organization or faculty search committee, only to find that unless you spend a substantial amount of time on each of these tasks, you will not accomplish any of these tasks. Certainly, it is not easy to let go of opportunities that were presented to you or that you personally sought out, for the sake of positioning yourself for the 'academic future' even if at the expense of your 'present.'

Work-life balance is broadly defined as one's ability to successfully carry out work and life. Although "successfully," can be distinctly conceptualized, work typically refers to professional responsibilities that are evaluated and rewarded. Life refers to social and personal concerns, such as family (Wheatley, 2012). Doc-

Beyond the Pride and the Privilege: The Stories of Doctoral Students and Work-Life Balance, pages xi–xv.

toral students spend most of their time fulfilling academic-related tasks, and in some instances, performing duties as graduate assistants. If they work full-time, they must multitask between assignments as students and duties as full-time employees. Their 'life' is often inundated with personal and professional activities that they have to allocate time to. Therefore, it is not uncommon that the life part is neglected and work becomes their life. Then life is only about work; which is not all encompassing of what life is meant to be. While it seems that being productive and dedicating most of your time for work is good, it can at the same time lead to a stressful life.

People's devotion to work has been widely recognized. Nearly half a century ago, Oates (1971) coined the term "workaholism" which refers to an addiction to spend a great deal of time working, to the extent of giving up social or recreational activities. This common compulsive behavior encouraged researchers to explore underlying reasons. The need for reward and recognition was one of the three motives of excessive work (Bonebright, Clay, & Ankenmann, 2000). In the case of doctoral students' whose typical work includes research and /or teaching, attending classes, working on class assignments, and dissertation writing, prioritizing work over everything else may be seen as obligatory, if not inevitable. It is part of earning the degree, as well as building one's resume; even when work 'disturbs' personal/family life and other activities.

Pursuing a doctoral degree is a privilege; and as the title of this book, *Beyond the Pride and the Privilege* suggests, oftentimes sacrifices or tradeoffs are necessary in order to survive and earn the highest academic degree, for most disciplines. This book presents an outlook of doctoral students' lives, which we hope will provide support to those who are working towards their doctoral degree as well as to those who aspire to enter the academic profession.

Autoethnography

Autoethnography is "an attempt to describe and analyze personal experience in order to explain cultural experience" (Ellis, Adams, & Bochner, 2010, p. 1). Known as a qualitative method that combines autobiography and ethnography, autoethnography is often used to write about past experiences that have impacted the course of current life (Denzin, 1989). Autoethnography gives the researcher the freedom to personalize writing in order to understand the social phenomenon (Wall, 2006). In writing an autoethnography, a researcher may pose questions to self and be mindful about the experience and how it influenced and shaped the current situation. Sheridan (2013) offered a list of prompts as a brainstorming process for autoethnographers, for instance, what I found inspiring about this study; the positive things from this experience; the frustrating things about this experience; how I feel about this experience; and what I learned from this experience.

In this book we utilized autoethnography as a method to tell the story of doctoral students' lives. Autoethnography allows each author to reflect on their life, to pause for a moment and think about how they make meaning of their work and life. Through autoethnography, readers can look into each author's life, and witness what is often overlooked and disguised underneath their status as doctoral students.

Diverse Population of Doctoral Students

The shifting landscape of higher education has opened the door of opportunity beyond the privileged few who tend to comprise students whose families have generationally obtained advanced degrees, have the financial security to pursue an advanced degree, and enter their program of study with limited responsibility other than to focus on their research agenda. In contrast to the traditional mold of yesterday's doctoral student, "young, White, single, male..." today's doctoral student reflects a broader scope of diversity (Gardner, 2008, p. 126). The profiles of the doctoral students represented as authors in this book have a rich demographic make-up, comprising single and married, young to middle-aged, parents—who may or may not be raising children alone, health conscious adults who are often part, or full-time employed individuals. This vast array of characteristics present unordinary tensions, propelling today's doctoral students to seek balance between their life, doctoral studies, and their various other commitments. *Beyond the pride and privilege: The stories of doctoral students and work-life balance* offers a glimpse into the inner workings of this new mold of student. Each author offers a compelling depiction of life negotiated within and beyond the academy. While some authors have chosen the route of graduate research assistant and full time student, others have chosen to maintain what one can equate to dual citizenship, of status within and outside of the academy, living parallel lives amidst the doctoral study workload.

These multi-faceted journeys have led a number of these authors to reflect on their personal wellness and the reality of the necessity of a focus on health. Thus, there are chapters that engage the reader in reflective practices to maintain a consciousness towards wellness. For example, James Vines writes about packing a lunch "in order to maintain a healthy diet" and attending a dance class twice a week on campus. He states, "Dancing is an excellent way to relieve stress, put the deadlines to the side for a while and have fun." On the other hand, Charlotte Evenson recognized: "Self-care was the first casualty of my survival..." These chapters contribute to the overall understanding of what doctoral students face in regards to work-life balance.

Other chapters shape the stories of doctoral students, who through their relatable experiences offer a vivid picture of what might be expected for the recently admitted doctoral student. Time is a precious commodity that is easily taken for granted until it is no longer available. The initial introduction into a doctoral study program is a quick reminder of this commodity. It is easy to be overwhelmed with writing assignments and readings that must be completed, and decisions must be made concerning where time can and should be allotted. Therefore, the stories in this book are insightful reflections and recommendations for students, for families that support them, and for professors concerned with understanding the doctoral student perspective. Each story provides a gracious plenty that can be devoured all at once or taken in small doses to assist in relating to the experience of work-life balance in the lives of doctoral students.

Why is the Doctoral Student Perspective Important in the Work-Life Balance Series?

In the first book of the series on work-life balance, *Juggling Flaming Chainsaws: Academics in Educational Leadership Try to Balance Work and Family*, Marshall et al. (2012) describes the lagging progress of the academy in restructuring to accommodate for the changing family. This, they explain, is due to labor market trends and the inclusion of "other conceptions of family" (p. xx). Furthermore, they state that changing families converge with the academy to create certain consequences for faculty. In turn, graduate students are less likely to seek faculty positions due to work-life balance incompatibility, resulting in a loss in human capital. Doctoral students are recognized as prospective faculty who are often mentored and nurtured as such through their programs of study. However, doctoral student attrition is a growing concern (Gardner, 2008; Golde, 2005). Fewer doctoral students results in fewer prospects for the professorship, impacting the academy. Institutions are expected to seek diverse professors reflective of the diverse student body, but a lack of attractiveness to the status of faculty launches a cyclical obstacle course where doctoral students do not want to seek the professoriate, the professoriate does not reflect the student body, and student attrition is impacted because professors are unable to relate to and retain the student body, which creates an overall impact on the academy. This is what can be referred to as the headbutt competition where nobody is a winner!

Doctoral Students: Adding to the Series on Work-Life Balance

Educational conferences are fertile ground for bridging innovative and clever ideas with opportunities for action. It was at the Annual Meeting of the American Educational Research Association Conference where the idea to add to the Work-Life Balance series from a doctoral student perspective was inspired. In the David L. Clark Scholars meeting, doctoral students shared research agendas and experiences that reflected what Marshall et al. (2012) describes as "the tension between the demands of work and [what she refers to as]… "not-work" (p. xiii). *Beyond the pride and the privilege: The stories of doctoral students and work-life balance* cultivated the soil bringing forth 21 chapters that contribute to the field of higher education from a number of different viewpoints. It includes the voices of multiple scholars from various walks of life. As illustrated in the autoethnography of Keith Cunningham, we are compelled to witness the challenging feats that he has experienced that, despite insurmountable difficulties, have not prevented him from advancing on the path to the doctorate. He details the changing terrain of his daily routine by sharing his wife's experience of "coming to grips with living with omnipresent pain and the potential for much greater disability in the future". Coming to grips with unintended changes in family status among other unexpected life events that alter one's path in the progression towards the doctorate are realities for far more than a few doctoral students, and as Leslie Shelton put it in her chapter, "This was NOT in the brochure!"

REFERENCES

Bonebright, C. A.,Clay, D. L., & Ankenmann, R. D. (200).The relationship of workaholism with work–life conflict, life satisfaction, and purpose in life. *Journal of Counseling Psychology, 47*(4), 469–477.

Denzin, N. K. (1989). *Interpretive biography*. Newbury Park, CA: SAGE.

Ellis, C., Adams, T. E., & Bochner, A. P. (2010). Autoethnografie. In G. Mey & K Mruck (Eds.), *Handbuch qualitative forschung in der psychologie* (pp. 345–357). Wiesbaden: VS Verlag/Springer.

Gardner, S. K. (2008). Fitting the mold of graduate school: A qualitative study of socialization in doctoral education. *Innovative Higher Education, 33*(2), 125–138.

Golde, C. M. (2005). The role of the department and discipline in doctoral student attrition: Lessons from four departments. *Journal of Higher Education, 76*(6), 669–700.

Marshall, J. M., Brooks, J. S., Brown, K. M., Bussey, L. H., Fusarelli B., Gooden, M. A., Lugg, C. A., Reed, L. C., & Theoharis, G. (2012). *Juggling flaming chainsaws: Academics in educational leadership try to balance work and family*. Charlotte, NC: Information Age Publishing.

Oates, W. E. (1971). *Confessions of a workaholic*. New York, NY: World Publication Company.

Sheridan, R. (2013, May 28). Autoethnography, an unusual research method, with the researcher as a participant. [Web log post]. Retrieved from https://confluence.cornell.edu/display/GOVT602/2013/05/28/Autoethnography%2C+An+Unusual+Research+Method%2C+With+the+Researcher+as+a+Participant.+By+Dr.+Rick+Sheridan%2C+Assistant+Professor%2C+Wilberforce+University

Wall, S. (2006). An autoethnography on learning about autoethnography. *International Journal of Qualitative Methods, 5*(2), 1–12.

Wheatley, D. (2012). Work-life balance, travel-to-work, and the dual career household. *Personnel Review, 41*(6), 813–831.

CHAPTER 1

REARRANGING MY PLATE

A Doctoral Journey

Paul Artale

The clock in my office reads 12:15 a.m. I am finishing the last of some truly terrible instant coffee while trying to figure out why my handouts for class are not printing. I will give the last presentation (that's for a grade anyway) of my academic career in eight hours. A few hours after that I will meet with my advisor to discuss my dissertation proposal. Oh crap! I forgot to update my literature review and refine my research questions! Add it to the list. Sleep is optional these days. Pity. In a few weeks I also become a father for the first time. Suddenly the line "Look at your life, look at your choices" begins to ring in to my head. And so I begin to reflect on this doctoral journey.

Years ago the only time I would have heard the words "Dr. Artale" would have involved some terribly imitated Austin Powers shtick. These days the term is heard more often and has an entirely different context. It is usually found in the question: "Hey Paul, how much longer until you become Dr. Artale?" My answer to that question is usually an incoherent chuckle followed by a shrug of my shoulders.

FROM PROFESSIONAL TO "GRAD"

Five years ago the idea of pursuing a doctorate in order to advance my career as a student affairs administrator did not exist. A conversation with a mentor at

Beyond the Pride and the Privilege: The Stories of Doctoral Students and Work-Life Balance, pages 1–7.

the National Association of Student Affairs Administrators in Higher Education (NASPA) conference changed all that; it planted the seed that inevitably led me to resign my job as Director of Residence Life and Judicial Affairs. I did not want to be a full time administrator working on my PhD. My work-life balance would suffer greatly as would the quality of my work in both the academic and professional domain. This marks the first time in my life where I became aware of the separation between work, family, and other endeavors. I had spent five years working 60–80 hour weeks as a student affairs administrator and football coach. I did not want to substitute the time I spent on a field, on the road, or in a film room with another endeavor. I love spending time with my wife and suddenly that became of paramount importance to me. Thus, I willingly gave up the status and thrill of running my own department for the life of a graduate assistant at another institution. It would allow me to spend more time with my family, finish the degree quicker, avoid debt, and increase the return on investment that was my PhD. Win-Win situation, right?

Don't get me wrong, I like what I do in student life. I am in charge of some great projects and advise phenomenal student leaders. My coworkers treat me like a professional and value what I add. That being said, I am still a graduate assistant and there are times when I struggle with no longer having true staff member status. Luckily I found development and professional collegiality through associations. These became a venue for me to network and in many cases, meet professionals who were either in my exact shoes or had been where I am at now. It offered both a way to help navigate this doctoral world and engage in professionally stimulating activities. Conferences have become a haven for me.

PERSONAL IDENTITY

Re-entry into the world of graduate studentdom caused me to struggle with who I was. If one were to look at me they would see a Caucasian male with a physical disability. I am missing fingers and have shortened forearms. My left hand resembles that of a Ninja Turtle while my right is more of a lobster claw. I am aware that I look different. The stares I get when I walk into a room or when the odd knucklehead refuses to shake my hand reminds me of that on a fairly consistent basis.

I do not strongly identify with being disabled. My Italian, Canadian, spousal, and athletic identities are far more dominant than the way I was born. Disability to me is an attitude and not a diagnosis. It does not define who I am and in terms of my doctoral identity, did not influence my research interests. I remember one of the first times my cohort sat around and discussed their research interests. As we went around the room it seemed people's research interests were tied to who they were and the experiences they had. My cohort mate with a finance background was interested in financial issues. My cohortmate who was Latino was interested in Latino/a issues. See a pattern? When it came time for me to discuss my interests I started talking about NCAA finance, employee burnout, and the business of education-nothing about being disabled. Over the course of my first year in the program there were instances, however, when people would approach me about conducting studies on disabled students or shifting my research in that direction. I respectfully declined.

My interests lay with issues of employee performance, academic capitalism, and so on. The closest my "disability" came to meshing with my student identity was getting angry at the lack of attention disabled students received in our student development class. There was not a single reading on the experience of disabled students in college or the different challenges those with physical disabilities face versus those with intellectual or psychological disabilities. For the first time in a long time, I was offended. I remember thinking "really, we study this population but nothing on disability" on a weekly basis. I should have spoken out, but I felt that if I did I would be married to the very identity I tend to disassociate myself from. I stayed silent, did my work, finished the course, and moved on with my life. Ironically, it is the "disabled" side of who I am that paved the way for me balancing my academic and social life.

WORK-LIFE AS A FIELD OF STUDY

By now you may be thinking "what does all this talk about identity have to do with work-life balance?" Three years ago I would have asked the same question. I have learned that identity and how we view ourselves has everything to do with balancing work and life. I had struggled with dissertation research topics ever since I entered my program. Athletic issues were too personal for me to be objective with. I found organizational and performance issues interesting but could never quite peg what part of it I was interested in. All I knew is that I had a healthy distaste for at-will employment and incompetent management. It made great material for a stand-up routine or blog but a little lacking for the direction I wanted to go; or so I thought. In my second year I did an independent study with a professor who was an expert in work-life balance. Everything clicked instantly. My biases, my interests, the problems I wanted fixed; all work life issues in some form from my perspective. Two readings into my independent study and I found a new passion and academic interest.

It was during the course of the readings that I learned about work-life boundaries. Our identities impact the quality of what we call work-life balance and lay the cornerstones of how we navigate the different roles we have in life. Some of us integrate our roles and are comfortable with mixing being a spouse, member of a cultural community, and manager without batting an eye. Integrators love the mix. That's not me. Some of us separate our roles and become angry and frustrated when one domain interferes with another. Suddenly being called into work during personal time is an example of this. Those who integrate would be fine with those, those who separate would see their blood pressure greatly increase. Finally there are volleyers who can shift between roles and identities if it is appropriate and expected. Blurring the lines is unacceptable except in certain circumstances or at certain times of year. That is totally me. I love to compartmentalize my identities and my roles but there are times where I have to accept that they will blend or not fit into neat little boxes. Thus, the disabled me belongs on a stage as a speaker not in the classroom as a lecturer. The moment I learned this I felt as if I had come into some rare and secret knowledge. When I looked at it from a professional standpoint I could see how an integrator boss could stress an integrator employee out.

So many times we see work-life as a scale that needs to be perfectly balanced. I was relieved to find out that doesn't have to be the case. If anything that is unrealistic. As I state in my seminars, work-life is more like a plate. Plates come in all shapes, sizes, colors, and patterns. Some have large areas to put your food in while others are almost more ornamental in nature. Some plates have dividers for the different foods we eat and the shape, size, and numbers of these compartments vary based on the design and in some cases compartments can be added/removed. In a nutshell we shape our plate based on our needs and our preferences. The plate analogy gave me a powerful tool to help me manage my personal life, my business, and frame my academic work. Win-win? Nah. This was an epic victory!

THE OTHER ME

"I say HIT, you say HARD! Let's try it." Is what I bellow at hundreds of people in an auditorium. "HIT!" and they yell back "HARD!" I repeat this a few more times before moving on to talking about how I was cut from the high school football team, only to find myself playing on a college field a few years later. I talk about perseverance, faith, never passing up opportunity, and surprisingly how to cope and overcome disability (which I define broadly). This is the start of the domain in my life that has become one of my key coping mechanisms in balancing school, family, work, and personal development: public speaking.

Paul Artale: Keynote Speaker and Leadership Facilitator is OK talking about disability and overcoming the odds. He also discusses work-life balance, leadership development, and how to become a more effective speaker. The fact that I can refer to my speaking persona in the third person is probably a sign of the significance this has to me....and that I may have an ego. Speaking has opened up a whole new world for me. I have since turned it into a side-business.

I fell into public speaking. During my first semester of my first year as a PhD student I joined a Toastmasters club to get some speaking experience. Toastmasters is an international organization with thousands of local chapters. The aim of Toastmasters is to improve the communication skills of its members whatever their level of comfort and experience is. In my first year as a Toastmaster, I had done decently on the local speech competition circuit and started to enjoy how liberating giving speeches could be. It wasn't because I have a talent for public speaking. What made my Toastmasters experience special was that it was an avenue where I didn't have to talk about class, my research interests, my post-graduation plans, or research about disabled students. Conversations were about regular things like what movies we had seen, mortgage rates, and the family members we loved (or tried to avoid). In the meeting room I was just Paul- a club member who likes to have fun. Meetings and competitions became a way for me to de-stress and just talk about whatever was on my mind. I could lay off NCAA politics and return to my Canadian roots by giving a goofy speech about Christmas in Canada. I met several people through Toastmasters, none of whom were in my PhD program and most of whom were not students. I quickly had a life outside of academe and I loved it!

I quickly took the lessons I had learned from joining Toastmasters and applied it to other aspects of my life. I became involved with other community organizations and events. When I connected with graduate student life it was almost always outside of my academic program. Michigan State has a fantastic Graduate Student Life and Wellness department. During my first year they would hold weekly coffee hours in my office building. My attendance at those events was strictly caffeine driven in the beginning. Quickly, I began to make acquaintances with other graduate students and together we could compare our experiences, vent if we needed to, and most importantly, take a break from the daily grind. Great friendships emerged from those coffee hours; many which still flourish today. This has been crucial in being able to deal with the stresses of doctoral life. It creates a special domain that on one hand can understand my frustrations and help me deal with them, and on the other hand provides a haven from the PhD process.

FAMILY LIFE

Early in this chapter I discussed the importance family life played in choosing my doctoral path. How ironic that I have waited until later in this chapter to discuss it. From a personal wellness and relationship perspective, my biggest fear in pursuing my PhD was not spending enough time with my wife. During the many doctoral orientation/admissions sessions I had attended in the previous year the theme of strained relationships and sacrifices being made to attain the degree became a constant theme. It scared me. I did not want my wife to resent me because of my academic work at the same time I wanted my life to be more than just my marriage and my work. I wanted a plate with lots of compartments even if some of those compartments were small.

I reacquainted myself with maximizing my pockets of free time. Bus rides became prime opportunities to complete readings as did times when my wife watched TV programs I had absolutely no interest in- I just can't get into Downton Abbey. Every minute was precious and I made sure I took advantage. My PhD work became a traditional Monday–Friday job. Weekends were strictly social and family time unless there was a good excuse for them not to be. I worked tirelessly to make sure that weekends stayed sacred. I am glad to say that my strategies and compartmentalized life worked well for me. I became so efficient that at times I was actually weeks ahead on some of my readings and projects. There were only a handful of late-night paper writing/reading sessions. All nighters were nonexistent. I have been fairly well rested during my doctoral experience. I was able to connect with family and friends, go on excursions, and give my marriage the proper attention it deserved.

My formula was running like a well-oiled machine for years one and two of my PhD program. By the summer of year two we had even managed to buy a house. Finances have always worried me as a graduate student, but through some frugal living and proper research we decided it would be prudent to buy a house in a fantastic neighborhood. Home ownership did not detract from my work-life endeavors, if anything it contributed to a more positive life. My screened in porch has become a nine month a year dwelling where I eat, entertain, and work. Writing on the back porch to the sounds of birds chirping, chipmunks chasing each other, and feeling the cool breeze on my face always manages to put my life into perspective. A visit from the occasional deer leads me to stop my work and watch them graze. It reminds me that no matter how important a task I think I am working on, balance and pleasure often comes from the simple things in life. Work can take a back seat even for a little while. It's O-K.

The third year in my program completely sabotaged my perfectly oiled work-life machine from the moment I learned I would soon be a father. My son would be due on May 6 (exam week). Suddenly, all of my priorities began to change. I struggled with this for a bit. The shape and compartments on my plate were going to morph into something completely different. The problem was that I had no idea what it should look like. I knew some things in my life would have to eliminated or reduced, but which ones and by how much? Through some deep conversations with family and self-reflection I decided to scale back my commitment to Toastmasters and other community organizations so that I could finish all of my coursework before the baby arrived. I would also reduce the amount of time spent on my speaking business to a handful of engagements; most of them were conference presentations I had already agreed to be at.

Spending weekends with my wife and friends did not change. The announcement of our pregnancy led to scores of people from the school community and our family supporting and helping us. Sometimes it was to donate items for the baby, at other times it was getting together and just having fun. This was needed in a year where so much of my time was spent on trying to finish coursework, finish a draft of my dissertation proposal, and earn extra money to offset medical expenses. It reinforced the importance of people in maintaining a positive work-life balance and led to me uttering words that three years prior I would have considered to be sinful: "It's just a PhD; other things need to come first right now."

Impending fatherhood led to me completely rearranging my life. I decided to sacrifice some of my balance in the short term (finishing coursework/adding an extra job) so that I could have more freedom in the long-term. I am ok finishing my degree later for the sake of family. I even turned down summer employment so that I can spend time caring for my son. The Paul of a year ago would have never considered that; money always had a large portion of the work-life plate.

12:45 A.M.

My materials are printed. Are they perfect? Not even close, but I am OK with that because the doctoral journey is a multidimensional process and not a linear path. During my time I have constantly (re)evaluated my priorities before ensuring that my actions and daily tasks reflected those priorities. Being centered in what is important to me has brought me peace, sanity, and balance. I have looked at my life, I have looked at my choices and aside from purchasing this terrible instant coffee, I am proud of this journey and how I've handled it. I know that Dr. Artale will emerge soon. When? (insert shoulder shrug) I am sure that will become a lot clearer when I look into my son's eyes for the first time.

CHAPTER 2

LEARNING TO INHALE

Charlotte Achieng-Evensen

The Walk

A breath in, a breath out
stingy sweat mopped down
a wide forehead, lashes stick together.
She lifts her foot, one step
a puff of air, three more minutes.
Her other foot raises up
she breathes in deeply
the foot comes down,
one minute.
She's walking to the end of time.
A step in front of a step
a skip over cracked sidewalks-
grass rising from within,
she steps again, verdant blades crushed
underneath, bleeding echoes of a remnant past
thirty seconds left,
thirty seconds…

Beyond the Pride and the Privilege: The Stories of Doctoral Students and Work-Life Balance, pages 9–15.

THE STARTING LINE

I began my studies with a shy excitement, a secret pleasure that I kept carefully protected. It seemed to me that participating in a doctoral program was a miraculous phenomenon, a treasured gift. I did not want the integrity of this opportunity compromised; therefore, I shared my plans with a very select group of people. My doctoral studies, after-all, were a goal that I had anticipated since my secondary school days. Encouraging external voices to comment on my academic goals would open up a space for jarring sideline discussion and obligate me to produce superficial responses. I was not ready for the insidious cynicism that would accompany such conversations. I wanted my passion for seeking knowledge to remain sweet and profound.

bell hooks (1994) writes, "I came to theory because I was hurting—the pain within me was so intense that I could not go on living" (p. 59). Like hooks, the journey into my PhD was an inevitable circumstance that began with my birth and formative years spent in East Africa. On the cusp of adolescence, my parents transplanted me into life within the United States. Along with a deeply established sense of self as a Luo tribal child, I had an equally rooted esteem for education, and the latitude for growth and achievement that it provided. I understood that knowledge would allow me the ability to pursue ambitions that I found meaningful. I understood, too, that as a young Kenyan girl, education would be key in this walk toward purpose.

hooks (1994) continues, "I came to theory desperate, wanting to comprehend—to grasp what was happening around and within me" (p. 59). As an African teenager in Southern California, there was no place of safety among my peers. I was rejected by my African American classmates because of my thick Luo-Swahili-tinged accent and by my dark skin color. Likewise, my White and Latino schoolmates did not accept me. I was too black, too ethnic, too everything different. Much like hooks, without theory, I could not understand this American world around me. I sought solace in books and found myself believing in this world of learning.

hooks (1994) adds, "most importantly, I wanted to make the hurt go away. I saw in theory then a location for healing" (p. 59). My identity as a learner and activist was then and is now, foundational to my idea of self. Indeed, I cannot remember childhood without the vision of me reading on my Grandfather's lap even as I listened to his discussions of the changes necessary for achieving public good. It was, therefore, a given that I felt incomplete without pursuing further schooling as a means of combating social issues. More poignantly, as I delved further into my career as a K-12 educator, I quickly recognized that I could not implement transformative action within my professional context because I did not understand the theoretical foundations of my praxis. I needed more schooling.

After weeks of applying and waiting, I received the coveted letter and enrolled in my chosen emphasis of Cultural and Curricular studies. An unusual feeling of homecoming accompanied my signature of intent to Chapman University. I had finally arrived from a long traveled journey. I, Charlotte Achieng, was a doctoral student ready to unpack myself fully into academics. I was ready to be submerged into the abundance of knowledge, the satisfaction praxis. Simply, I was ready to fall in love.

This euphoric feeling carried me through the first weeks of the semester. I imagined myself a conqueror like my ancestral warrior-uncles. As fall classes continued, my joy dissipated and I found myself humbled. I felt consummately defeated and spent countless moments wallowing in perpetual confusion. This was not a gradual, expansive experience like wading into a warm, shallow pool. Rather, it was a desperate galvanizing reaction to the continual overload of information pouring over and into me. I had not expected that delving into theory would require opening my soul and examining my stance, privileges, knowledge, and lack thereof. I was not prepared for the psychological impact of being immersed in profound thought for seemingly endless amount of continual hours. Nor was I ready for the cognitive demands of deconstructing the world around me and preparing somewhat cogent responses to it. I constantly questioned the emergence of any actual meaning from the lessons that I was learning within the program. I questioned whether or not my identity as a learner and a social change agent remained viable. Most importantly, I questioned the validity of undergoing such stringent intellectual practice as a means of effecting practical change for my students and my community.

ESTABLISHING A PACE

The genesis of my entry into the academy required a steep intellectual, social, and emotional learning curve that mandated a critical re-training of my knowledge base. It required, too, the discipline of solitude. I had to be alone in the metacognitive processes of my learning, My studies isolated me within my life. This early lesson became apparent in my work as a teacher and in my personal life.

As one who has spent the past 15 years teaching secondary school I worked to maintain an open door policy for my students. They could come and go into my classroom as they pleased. For them, I was available before, during, and after school. Within the first month of PhD studies, I recognized that this policy was no longer possible. Aside from the fact that I left the school campus immediately when the last class bell rang in order to attend my afternoon doctoral classes, I now had to institute office hours. This was a challenge for my young students, especially those struggling with the stringency of time management and organization.

I remember particularly, Edwin, a ninth grade student athlete. As the result of a middle school experience that did not require extraneous academic effort on his part, Edwin had not developed strong study habits. On the eve of an important game, Edwin rushed to my classroom to make up his missed assignments. He arrived just as I was locking the door, and I could not help him. Consequently, he missed his game and began to lose hope in his ability to achieve academic success. While I could argue that Edwin learned a valuable life lesson regarding the necessity of organization and motivation, I was disheartened. In front of me stood a young man caught in the transitional dilemmas that plague middle and high-schoolers. More and more, I began to feel that I was not providing enough support to my struggling students. I was becoming alienated from the foundational motivation that drove me into pursuing my doctorate. Instead of drawing closer to my professional purpose as an educator, I was cultivating an unspoken chasm. Ironically, my class schedule limited the time I had to interact with the very students who I sought to serve.

These lessons of isolation continued in my personal life. I could no longer participate in family and social gatherings. If the occasion was not direly significant, I did not attend. My attention was sequestered to books and engulfed in my writing. My generally open phone line became a filled voicemail box of calls to be returned at some unspecified date. Whenever that date arrived, I was fraught with a volatile cocktail feeling-mixture of guilt, shame, and resentment. The guilt and shame rose from maintaining poor, limited relationships with those closest to me. The resentment was built upon a latent hostility which emerged from my un-communicated need for support. I sensed that my support system did not value my intellectual and emotional struggles even though I had not clearly articulated this need. The more heavily I engaged in seeking knowledge through coursework, the more the social support that buoyed my identity as a passionate learner began to crumble. Purpel (1999), in a critique of higher education writes, "we for the most part believe we can forge a life of justice and joy through highly developed rational, analytical, and creative understanding" (p. 15). This, indeed was my belief and my practice. But, as my studies distanced me from community and I fell into emotionally murky territory, I began query this belief. Furthermore, I began to doubt the validity of the academic landscape I had endeavored to join. I sought intervention.

LEARNING TO INHALE

Slowly, an intuitive truth seeped into my consciousness. I began to understand that I was holding my breath. That is, I was no longer allowing myself to fully experience my humanity. According to Freire (1970/2000), "we are beings in the process of *becoming*" (p. 85). We are thoroughly immersed in a dialectical social experience with our holistic selves, our community, and our environment. Recognizing this, I began to understand that I was straining to find the space to breathe, to live.

In those first months as a graduate student, I found myself in constant and intense motion. I was caught in the structure of the academic system and found myself interacting with the world that propelled me on a high-speed intellectual obstacle course that offered no reprieve. Ensnared in the spinning wheels, I was falling all the while assuming that I was the failure. Between work and school, social life and community, I craved air—the ability to simply *be*. I needed rest and this could come only with a purposeful space for *resting.* Yet, that very concept of creating a habit of rejuvenation seemed to be anathema to my academic progress. My doctoral studies dictated a life parceled out into managed segments, all of which I juggled in the order of perceived immediacy. For a woman whose true home is the highly relational and fluid context of Africa, such inflexible rigidity enervated my soul. Moreover, it led me into a self-reflexive examination of my purpose for pursing a doctorate.

At this juncture, I started to examine the contradictions that I faced: the pursuit of higher education curtailed the creativity of my teaching practice; the solitude required for my studies meant that I neglected my social relationships, and so forth. Eventually, I was forced to rearticulate the purpose of my education. Doctoral studies, I reasoned, allowed me the resources to enact transformative change within my professional and social contexts. However, these studies were not the only important priorities in living meaningfully. I needed a more holistic, balanced approach. Having arrived at this conclusion, I created a pattern for engagement with my academic pursuits. I called it my survival blue-print.

My professional life was the first segment within the blueprint that required review. I recognized that my vocation, along with its various responsibilities, required that I remain available to students, parents, and staff. The second segment encompassed interactions with my social community. The third segment was that of self-care. In this place, I planned for exercise and diet, well-being and meditation, sleep and rest. The final segment in my survival blue-print, and the one battling all other areas, was the vortex of graduate studies.

In a critical examination of this barren land, I excavated clear evidence of how I had become consumed with studying. Each week, I was immersed in volumes of reading and endless writing tasks. Delving into the literature I found the abundance of information to be both exhausting and exhilarating. The constant demand to produce intelligent and provoking knowledge was taxing. I realized, too, that scholarship did not end with mining through books. There implicit expectations for scholarly engagement demanding attention. As a part of my studies, I was required to participate in my learning community. I had to be involved in writing groups with my colleagues, and to present at conferences. I was expected to volunteer, teach, and contribute to the academy through quantifiable and specific scholarly tasks. In addition, it became apparent that in this arena, my K-12 experience was not considered intellectually sufficient. Quickly, I realized that my survival blue-print need more than organization. It needed a holistic approach.

KEEPING PACE—FINDING BALANCE

The work-life imbalance that I encountered in my first year of doctoral studies was not due to a lack of mindfulness. I was, quite simply, overwhelmed by the explicit and implicit demands of the academy. Scholarly engagement, along with coursework, required a level of sustained intellectual and emotional focus that surprised me. Indeed, the very fact of this surprise sent me into further distress.

For the first time in my academic career, I felt utterly inadequate and I was demoralized. Instead of focusing my energies toward deciphering dense theory, I found myself battling emotions that accompanied my perceived failure. On both the academic and personal fronts, I was losing. Although I had created a survival blue-print for achieving my goals, I had not yet achieved a viable rhythm in my daily life. My system began collapsing.

Self-care was the first casualty of my survival blue-print because it lacked external, immediate repercussions. At first, I reasoned that I could always catch up on my sleep. Next, exercise became optional. Soon, my eating habits suffered. I attempted to make healthy eating choices, but I could not find the time to plan my meals. Vague memories of super-market aisles were replaced with the neon veneers of restaurants and the inconstant drum of local coffee shops. Finally, with self-care uncomfortably and temporarily shelved, I found myself jumping furiously between excellence at work and excellence at school. My bursts of productivity were fueled with awkward spurts of wonderful achievement and equally shameful guilt. I was on a predictable pendulum. I was simultaneously saddened that I could not spend more time with my students, and really excited about the most current theorist I discovered. Then, I became passionate about using newly learned strategies in the classroom, yet I found my performance in doctoral scholarly engagement mediocre. So it went. I was a confused, agitated individual attempting to find equilibrium. I needed a more livable plan.

Upon rumination, I discovered that the connective theme in my struggles was time. As much as I disliked it, I was a commodity of the academy, and I needed to learn how to engage my inner resources within a system that was destroying me. I needed to learn how to reclaim my humanity. Armed with this knowledge, I re-sketeched my survival blue-print. Instead of prioritizing my activities by tasks, I began to think spatially. That is, I embraced the notion of time as space. Within this space, I could construct, create, and mediate the different spheres of my life. I was no longer at the whim of external expectations. I could manage and choose my involvement.

As with all spaces, it was crucial to consider practical parameters for organization. Almost casually, I arrived at the thought, *twenty minute increments.* The idea came after a particularly brutal week left me feeling that I had not served my students, family, or schooling well. Determined to relax, I decided to complete a twenty minute exercise video. This commitment did not feel like a heavy burden. It was not, for example, a one hour gym session that would have sent me into existential panic. The levity that accompanied my workout session led me to a new life mantra- *twenty minute increments*. I incorporated it, loosely, as the base of my survival blue-print and foundation for balancing my life. This idea of time—as a space—began to influence my life management. Each task became a twenty minute block with margins of time placed as buffers before and after. In this way, no one task felt overwhelming, and the boundaries created by my studies became manageable. I began to maintain a relatively balanced life.

THE SPACE TO BREATHE

I entered my doctoral studies with the certainty that I was embarking upon important work. Quickly, it became evident that such study can be contradictive. That is, even though the end goal of my scholarship was to contribute toward societal progress, my journey in the learning was much akin to a solitary, lonely walk. I was alone with my books, alone with my thoughts, and alone in my writing. In the process of my studies, I found myself changing from an engaged member of society into a disconnected stranger within my own life. I realized that I needed habits that allowed me to remain holistically involved in the world.

In response to this need, I created a survival blue-print. It, however, did not alleviate my desperate sense of drowning because I found myself mercilessly wedded to a schedule. Each day was planned meticulously, without much room for deviation. Consequently, I became my own enemy, struggling intimately with my purpose for joining the academy as well as the fear of wavering from the goal of completing my studies. Through a reflexive process and painful experience, I arrived at a position of balance in my work, studies, and life. This new rhythm involved a comprehensive, more relational interaction with time as space.

In this space, I have the ability to move fluidly toward full engagement within the academy without wholly sacrificing the community that shores me and keeps me hopeful. Most importantly, I am able to cultivate habits that maintain my passion as a learner and my goals as a transformative social agent. Although incremental success comes with waves of minor failures, I can finally bring myself fully to the task of scholarship. I have found the space to breathe. Finally, I can inhale.

REFERENCES

Freire, P. (1970/2000). *Pedagogy of the oppressed.* New York: Continuum.

hooks. (1994). *Teaching to transgress: Education as the practice of freedom.* New York: Routledge.

Purpel, D. E. (1999). *Moral outrage in education.* New York: Peter Lang.

CHAPTER 3

FLYING, FALLING, AND THE SPACE BETWEEN

David M. Brown

Remember falling off your bike as a kid? There was a particular sensation in those moments after you had fallen off but before you hit the ground—a scary, thrilling weightlessness that you hoped wouldn't end in disaster. That's how I would describe being a doctoral student. Sure, there are occasional bursts of exhilaration when, like riding over the crest of a big hill, the hard work is done and for an instant you can take your feet off the pedals and just enjoy the ride. But mostly it's that other feeling—that sense of flying and falling and the faith that somehow everything will be okay. I believe it's the willingness to endure that sensation, for years on end, that carries students successfully through their programs. Though we share a capacity to persevere, to rise to the challenges of our respective programs, each of us is led to pursue a doctoral degree by circumstances that are uniquely our own. For me, the decision to embark on the path to a PhD was about discovering a passion that had been hiding in plain sight.

WAKING UP

Without my realizing it, I had been feeling the pull of academia long before I enrolled in my current program. For several years after we married, my wife and I

Beyond the Pride and the Privilege: The Stories of Doctoral Students and Work-Life Balance, pages 17–21.

crisscrossed the country on summer road trips in a quest (since completed) to visit all 50 states. On those trips, I noticed that the places to which I was drawn often seemed to have colleges and universities nearby. Even in the summer, college towns hum with a particular sort of energy. It was wondering about the nature of that hum and trying to understand what about it appealed to me in such a profound way that kindled my interest in higher education. I began to read everything I could lay my hands on about higher education and its history; pretty soon, I was hooked. I was ready to make a change, ready to trade my cushy but mind-numbing public sector job for the thrill of scholarship; all I needed was a catalyst—something to push me in the right direction. It came in the form of an acceptance letter to a doctoral program. It's a storybook ending, right? Man finds his passion, goes off to graduate school, and lives happily ever after? Not exactly—there was one small catch: that letter wasn't mine.

As I was weighing my options for continuing my education, my wife had been planning the next step in her own career. While I was still contemplating the idea of applying to a doctoral program, she was actually doing it. We had discussed in a superficial way what we would do if she got in, but mostly we just kicked the can down the road; "Let's worry about it if it happens" was a common refrain around our house in those days. My wife didn't have to tell me that she'd been accepted—the gasp and the flailing arms pointing to her computer screen let me know as much. And just like that, our adventure had begun. A few months later, on a sweltering August afternoon in 2009, she loaded up her car and waved goodbye, bound for the University of Kentucky (UK).

Once the prospect of my wife returning to school had gone from a hazy possibility to a plan in motion, I began plotting my own leap into academia. I continued to work; nurturing a nest egg that I hoped would keep us financially afloat through what promised to be several lean years. I filled my time with books and journal articles on higher education, anxiously awaiting the day when I, too, would be Kentucky-bound. Over those next few months, frequent visits to Lexington and the UK campus were bittersweet; they were two- or three-day tastes of the life I longed to have. With each visit, the siren call of campus life grew more enchanting. Finally, the months of anxious waiting came to an end; I was admitted to UK's doctoral program in higher education the following spring. Wide-eyed and eager to set the scholarly world ablaze, I arrived in Lexington in the summer of 2010. I was ready to begin a new life.

KEEPING TIME

As it turned out, living in different states was excellent preparation for the rhythm of married life for two doctoral students. In the course of that year apart, the tempo of my wife's day-to-day schedule as a busy student became our new norm; even as I continued to plod through my 9–5 routine, the ebbs and flows of her life as a doctoral student and all its attendant obligations were how we kept time. We developed a routine during the week—a phone call in the morning, sporadic text messages during the day and a regular time late each evening when we would video chat. We economized our words, condensing stories and distilling ideas to fit the little time we had. Living under the same roof again once I moved to Kentucky, we fell effortlessly into an almost identical routine as the new academic year began: a conversation every morning (in the car as we drove to campus), periodic messages during the day and a chat every night recounting the day's highs and lows. Weekends, though more laid back, were (and often still are) passed in long stretches of silence, with my wife on one end of the couch and I at the other as we work through our respective piles of journal articles or papers to grade. Every once in a while, sometimes without even looking up, one of us will reach over and squeeze the other—an unspoken way of saying, "I'm busy, and you're busy, but we're in this together. I'm glad you're here."

OFF THE CLOCK

One of the quirks of graduate education is that time takes on a different meaning. Even activities that aren't directly related to scholarship are still measured in those terms. For doctoral students, time is often measured by what one is (or ought to be) accomplishing. Hours and minutes lose their significance; instead, time is calculated in articles read, grant applications written, and conference proposals submitted. Something as simple as an invitation to go out to dinner can set off an internal struggle of epic proportions: What won't get crossed off my to-do list if I go? Who's going to be there—anyone I can network with? Is it worth the extra work I'll have to do tomorrow?

Other than fellow students, few understand the time-intensive nature of a doctoral program. Perhaps that's why virtually all of the friendships that I've developed in my time at UK have been with other doctoral students. They understand the value of having a night off to have a few drinks and eat things that don't come with instructions that say, "Heat on high for 90 seconds." Socializing with other students can be profound; to see half a dozen of the most driven and intelligent people you know dissolve into maniacal laughter over a crude joke is cathartic and wonderful in ways that defy easy explanation. Simple pleasures like sharing a meal remind us that it's important to leave books unopened or undergrads' papers ungraded, even if just for a night, to engage in the sorts of things that "normal" people do. My research focuses on student life and how much of the college experience takes place outside of the classroom; in my own life I am reminded that that holds true, even for graduate students. Nights passed sitting around a homemade fire pit in a fellow student's front yard have, in their own way, been just as valuable to me as days spent in the classroom. What I've learned over the past three years about being a scholar, a teacher, and a researcher has been complemented and strengthened by the virtues I've seen demonstrated by my peers: humility, wit, determination, and an appreciation for the simple joys of the pauper-scholar existence.

TENDING THE MIND-BODY CONNECTION

Remembering to set aside time for friends is only part of the equation for students' wellbeing; for all of the demands that a doctoral program makes on the mind, it can also take a toll on the body. Hours spent in front of the computer or hunched over a desk reading pages of miniscule type may sharpen the intellect, but they can also bring aching joints, flabby limbs, and a waistline intent on growing. I discovered during my first stint in graduate school that exercise was an important part of coping with the pressures of working on an advanced degree. Kickboxing and yoga carried me through an MBA program, and it didn't take long once I started working on my PhD to remember why those things were so important. Early in my program, I took up running as a way to keep stress at bay. Beyond the obvious physical benefits, running reminds me to carve out a place in my day where it's okay to take a step back from things and let my mind wander. I haven't quite reached the point where I can turn my brain off during a run and leave problems untended for the space of an hour or two, but I don't mind that; running isn't so much an escape for me as it is a different way to process the contents of my head. Many of the problems that I've encountered—the little defeats and frustrations that crop up in a doctoral program—don't seem nearly as daunting when they're set to the tune of feet thumping on pavement. Oh, how easily worries melt and good ideas bubble to the surface in the middle of a good, long run!

BRANCHING OUT

Beyond cultivating one's mind and body, an important aspect of the doctoral student experience is a willingness to embrace new challenges. One of the goals I set for myself when I went back to school was to step outside of my comfort zone and look for new ways to grow. To that end, the most pleasant surprise of my time as a doctoral student has been discovering a passion for teaching. Just when I thought I had reached a sort of equilibrium, my department offered me the opportunity to become a teaching assistant. For the past two years I have taught an undergraduate course called "Education in American Culture"—an experience that has proven to be challenging and rewarding in ways I could not have imagined. To say that I was out of my comfort zone when I began comically understates the trepidation I felt; faced with teaching two sections of a full-responsibility course, my comfort zone wasn't even within shouting distance! I am forever indebted to those students whom I had that first semester—they bore my esoteric jokes and earnest, if not always contagious, enthusiasm with patience beyond their years. Eventually, I found my bearings, and with them a joy and sense of satisfaction unlike anything else I have known.

Mindful that confidence is no substitute for competence, I have sought out ways to bolster my teaching skills; the same semester I began teaching I became involved with my university's Preparing Future Faculty program. Both personally and professionally, it has proven to be a valuable and worthwhile endeavor. While my teaching has certainly benefitted from my participation, perhaps the greatest value of the program has been meeting doctoral students in other disciplines—everything from biology and chemistry to literature and art. Getting to know them and seeing the ways in which they try to strike their own work/life balances has been eye-opening. It is easy in higher education to become compartmentalized—to keep to ourselves and forget about the department down the hall or on the next floor or on the other side of campus. Though there are certainly plenty of differences between our fields, what I have been struck by most with those students is the degree to which our experiences are *the same.* A rejected conference proposal feels as bad to a scientist as it does to an educator. A publication, no matter the field, no matter how far down in the "et al." one's name is buried, is a cause for celebration! I have friends who go to conferences I've never heard of to discuss topics that don't interest me, but I share in their excitement because I know what the stakes are—I know the hours they've put in and I am thrilled to see their efforts rewarded. To be a doctoral student is to gain admission to a club of strange and wonderful people whose successes can embolden us and whose disappointments can hurt as much as our own. We root for each other because somehow a victory for one of us feels like a victory for all of us—a reminder that the hard work we're doing will eventually pay off.

EQUILIBRIUM

When I first started thinking about how to write about my work-life balance, my first thought was, "No problem—I've got a great balance!" But as I reflected on my time in my program and set about writing this chapter I realized that that wasn't true—or, at least, it wasn't the whole truth. It isn't that my life is perfectly balanced—far from it. But I think that balance is a matter of perception; is it still "work" if it doesn't feel like work? As I finish up my final year of coursework and prepare for my qualifying exams, I find that my enthusiasm for studying higher education has not diminished. It has taken me many years, but as I stroll happily through my mid-thirties, I am confident that I've found my equilibrium. I tell my students at the end of every semester that if they find the thing that they love to do, it won't feel like work. On that point, I am happy to say I can speak from experience.

CHAPTER 4

LIVING TO LEARN AND LEARNING TO LIVE

A Story of Perspective, Professionalism, Purpose, and Perseverance

Melissa R. Byrne

> It's 2:00 AM and the only light on in my two-bedroom condo is the light of my computer screen. I am not only staring at my computer screen, but staring through it as I struggle to arrive at just the right title for my dissertation; To use a colon or not? What is the benefit of using a question mark in the title? How do I use quotation marks to emphasize just the right word? What if my professor doesn't like my topic? Am I still on track with my timeline? Wait, did I let my dogs out tonight?

I was in the midst of my first year as a doctoral student and the task of choosing a dissertation topic that was just the right fit seemed like an insurmountable task at the time. How was I supposed to settle on just one narrow topic to dedicate the next several years of my life to? Since it was 2:00 in the morning, landing on the perfect title would seem silly to most; however, those who are going through the same process know exactly what I mean. To me, having the perfect title was everything. I somehow could not convince myself to continue writing until I had a

Beyond the Pride and the Privilege: The Stories of Doctoral Students and Work-Life Balance, pages 23–29.

title that stuck. In a moment of panic, I picked up my phone and called my friend of 13 years, Tommy, who is a year ahead of me in the process. He picked up the phone and I immediately start rattling off my different dissertation titles. Tommy gently said, *"You do know that I am leaving for India in the morning and I still need to pack?"* And I respond with, *"Yes, I know, but I am meeting with my professor tomorrow, so I need to figure this out!"*

The journey of being a doctoral student is one that I could have never imagined before I actually experienced it. I was prepared for a great deal of work and learning, but I was completely unprepared for the journey that was ahead of me. What do I mean by completely unprepared? I knew that I was about to embark upon the most challenging academic experience of my life, but I had no idea how much I would change as a person as a result of the process. My entire life, education has been a top priority to me. I was a first generation college graduate, so not only did I owe it to myself to earn a degree, but I hoped that through earning a degree, I could help pave the way for future generations of my family and serve as a role model and show that no goal or dream is too big. As I continued to go to school, my hunger for learning became stronger and stronger. My thirst for knowledge was never quenched, as I always yearned to see the big picture beyond the walls of individual classrooms; investigating the systems and structures that move larger numbers of students in ways that truly transform, ignite, and inspire young minds through new innovative pedagogical strategies. I dreamt of the day that I would be Dr. Melissa Byrne, not because of the title, but because of the potential that it had for innumerable students whom I have yet to meet; but it always seemed so far away, so tedious, and sometimes so overwhelming that I lost sight of the finish line, only able to focus on the road directly at my feet. What helps to get me through the experience of being a doctoral student while maintaining work-life balance are perspective, professionalism, purpose, and most importantly, perseverance.

PERSPECTIVE

I came into the doctoral program expecting to learn deeply and open my mind to the bigger picture in curriculum and instruction. Even though I was less than a year out of my master's program, I knew that I needed to learn more and produce *something* that would affect change for a larger audience and publish research that actually mattered in the lives of real students. Little did I know that even though my motivation was for an audience outside of myself that I in turn would be embarking on a transformational journey that would forever change me as an educator, administrator, scholar, and person. I have learned that the relationships established with fellow doctoral students and professors are crucial. Meaningful relationships make the difference between struggling to survive the process or truly embracing the experience of growing into and accepting the responsibilities that come with being a scholarly practitioner. When it seems impossible to maintain a work-life balance, your fellow students and professors are the ones who show you that it *is* possible to work full-time, hold crazy hours, and somehow hold your eyelids open long enough to get those next few articles read and put your thoughts to paper-even if those dishes stay in the sink just a while longer. On the days that there don't seem to be enough hours in the day and you can't seem to stomach another cup of coffee, look to those who have been there before you because they are living proof that you, too, *can* do this. Your professors are the ones who have been there before you; both as doctoral students themselves, but also as experienced guides through the doctoral process. Truly, they have paved the way for other doctoral students and are there for you to ensure you make it through. Lean on them, ask them questions, and send them your 27 article summaries to make sure you are on the right track. What I have come to realize is that this really boils down to trust. Trust that your countless hours of work and dedication will not be in vain; that if you are veering down a rabbit hole, that you will be guided back to the path toward graduation. And, if you are as lucky as me, you are part of an educational institution that refuses to let students slip through the cracks and is dedicated to help transform the next generation of educators into people who are able and willing to change the system in order to ensure that all students are able to succeed.

One of the most challenging, rewarding, but also most gut-wrenching parts of the doctoral process is forming your dissertation committee. My first year in the program, I had multiple wonderful professors who I learned a great deal from, but choosing the faculty member who would be just the right fit as chair is a process that should not be taken lightly. In the summer of my first year, I had the opportunity to take a course about culture and diversity that pushed me to new limits by challenging me to rethink what I thought I knew about education. While I had taken similar courses in the past, through the course content I knew I could never be the same. Also, I knew that this faculty member was *meant* to be my dissertation chair. It was as if the stars were aligned. After establishing a great deal of trust and mutual respect for one another, I formally asked my professor to chair my committee, which she graciously accepted. We met frequently throughout the summer and into the fall to refine my topic, revise my proposal drafts, and dream about the impact that this research would have for my field. I believed I was on track to defend my proposal by the end of winter of my second year. It was perfect.

As with everything that has been planned and plotted to perfection, I learned that plans are only that, and can change quicker than they were put into place. In fact, the stars were not aligned and my chair would not be on my committee. In fact, she would be leaving the university at the end of the semester. This was a hard pill to swallow, like trying to swallow a cantaloupe in one gulp. While it seems extreme now, there were tears—lots of tears. What was I going to do now? After the emotions ran their course, it became clear that it was time for 'Plan B,' I wasn't going to quit; I needed to start looking for a new dissertation chair. While I wondered how I could possibly find another chair who could start where my previous chair left off, with the support of my former chair, I found an experienced, knowledgeable, dedicated, and witty professor to take over the role of chair, whom I have now put my trust in as I continue my journey towards my doctorate. Not only did I think my new chair would be effective, but having received my undergraduate degree from the same university, my new chair knew me as a learner. Anyone who knows me knows that it is extremely important because being challenged and pressed to do better is how I learn best. Despite what I thought was an earth-shattering change, I was able to pick myself up and hit the ground running (maybe walking at some points) with my proposal. The reason that I tell this story is that having perspective in an experience such as this is vital. When you think your world is crashing down around you, it is extremely important to know and understand that it will be okay. Breathe. Cry if you need to. And remember that even if it is difficult to see at the time, you will get through this and more importantly learn from it. The world will only end if you let it. The lesson of gaining and maintaining perspective has continually allowed me to achieve a true balance. True balance is feeling a sense of calm in the midst of it all, being in a state of flow, reaching out to your support people when you need to, and trusting in the process. I believe that having perspective is a choice. I had to choose to move forward with the circumstances that I had been dealt, even if it was not in my plans. Now, I am very aware that some things are out of my control and that I have to trust that everything always works out, provided that I make the effort to reframe my expectations of *how* I will reach the end goal. Not *if* I reach it, how.

PROFESSIONALISM

By day, I am Assistant Director of Curriculum for a large unit school district in the western suburbs of Chicago. As a curricularist, the hours are long and mentally intense and critical thinking is required nearly every moment of my day. Despite the assignment that is due, reading that I should have done, and laundry that still won't wash itself, I have to be fully engaged in my work if I am to effectively impact the lives of the learners whom I so deeply care about. Finding a true work-life balance has sometimes been a struggle because both work and school are priorities, but there is only one me. There is always a meeting to attend, a deadline to meet, and a paper to write. With only 24 hours in a day, some days it doesn't seem humanly possible to stay on track with everything, but it is crucial to maintain professionalism at all times, whether Melissa the professional or Melissa the student. Fortunately, my position as Assistant Director of Curriculum has afforded me the opportunity to incorporate my professional experiences into my doctoral studies and vice versa. Being a doctoral student has made me a much more effective curriculum specialist, as I am able to apply new learning every day in my professional role. What I've learned is that it is okay, even ideal to *double-dip.* As opposed to seeing my work and school as opposing, even competing forces, I have learned to maximize the extent to which I can use my professional experience to strengthen my scholarship, and vice versa. This is what I am learning is the life of a scholarly practitioner.

PURPOSE

Everyone thinks of his or her purpose in life. Or at least I think they do. I hope they do. Seeking and knowing your purpose is an important part of the journey. I know that for me, identifying my purpose, even writing it down, has been a source of strength and encouragement during times of frustration, stress, defeat, and inevitable recovery. While all of our senses of purpose may be different, I believe that mine is to equip and evoke transformation in others, so that they can embrace themselves as loving, loved, and capable individuals; for whom dreams are possible and no feat is too great. I am honored (and often humbled) to be one of the volunteer directors for a high school leadership program that focuses on drug, alcohol, and suicide prevention. Volunteering for this program is my soul food. Being surrounded by books, theory, APA, and stacks of articles, I sometimes lose myself in the reality that the world is still spinning and that there are important things that deserve love and attention (that are not my dissertation) and being a part of this remarkable program brings me back to life. When beginning an EdD or PhD program, many will tell you of the importance of taking time for yourself or being involved in things other than your dissertation. Giving back and being there for others is part of what keeps me grounded. The teens in the program give me hope for the future and knowing that I might make a difference in one person's life makes it all worthwhile. It is my involvement in this program that has brought me to the most genuine, dependable, and trusted friends a person could ask for. They know me and see me as more than an educator or student; they see me as a person and not just a research paper producing machine. Each and every day, I am grateful for the unwavering support that I have in my trusted friends. At the end of the day, when looking at all that needs to get done and deadlines that need to be met, I can never lose sight of my purpose and the importance of my relationships with others because that is what truly matters.

PERSEVERANCE

In addition to gaining perspective, maintaining professionalism, and knowing my purpose, I have learned that it is truly perseverance that will see me through to the day I defend my dissertation and stand in front of my advisor at the hooding ceremony. There have been many times that I yearn to take that bike ride or watch that missed episode of *Modern Family*; however, time and time again, I load up my backpack and head to the local coffee shop for a lengthy study and writing session. Even though "relaxing" might not be on the agenda for the next several years, I have learned to appreciate the small things and be more present in the moment. I have stopped pining over dissertation titles, trusting that the right one will come in time. Setting goals and staying connected is important for me as I strive to maintain a work-life balance. Setting a daily reading and writing goal is a must. Whether you prefer time writing or words written, it is important to set a goal and stick to it.

In persevering through the doctoral program and dissertation process, I have had to look deeply at my relationship with my longtime friend, perfection. Perfection is both a blessing and a curse, especially in the dissertation process. I have learned that through striving for perfection, that same thirst for perfection can paralyze you in fear of making mistakes. I have found myself many times reworking a paragraph for hours to get "just the right wording" or mulling over the way your dissertation research will change the work in your field, only to look back at your computer screen and realize you have only written one paragraph in two hours. I constantly have to remind myself that Anne Lamott was right, a sh*%&y first draft is fine, and good work is done "bird by bird." Your dissertation does not have to change the world. Yes, it needs to be innovative, unique, and useful, but remember that it is the first chapter in your life as a scholar, not the last. Finding a comfortable study setting is important, too. Whether it is permanently "reserving" a table at your local coffee shop and surrounding yourself with other scholars or creating a place of solitude at your home with a desk and supportive desk chair, having a study place that you can call yours is key. Setting goals helps to not only achieve a work-life balance, but maintain it as well. Having goals allows me to stay on target and each goal I reach is a small win, which deserves to be celebrated, even with a night off.

What gives me the strength to persevere is the support that I have around me. I would not be who I am today without my "balcony people," the ones who are always there for me without fail, who have believed in me every step of the way, rejoice in my successes, and are there to catch me when I fall. Sitting and talking over a cup of coffee with a trusted friend makes the world of difference; talking to those who have walked the path before me and hearing it will be okay helps me press on. Knowing that I have unwavering support and friendship around me gives me the strength I need to get through and even flourish through this process. I am forever grateful for the friendship, love, and support that comes from my balcony people every day, for it gives me the strength to persevere and maintain a work-life balance. Throughout the journey of being a doctoral student, there have been wonderful days, challenging days, happy days, and sad days, but I would not trade even the worst of them because that would alter the experience that has forever changed me into not only the person I want to be, but the person I am *meant* to be.

CONCLUSIONS

Living a busy and fast-paced life prior to the doctoral experience, I tended to go from one thing to the next as if checking things off of a "to-do" list. That was not the person I wanted to be. I had so many people and experiences that were so important to me, I was afraid I would miss out on the journey of life. When I started this program, I began to realize that it wasn't just taking the classes, completing the readings, and writing the dissertation that mattered; it was also just as much about the experience and the journey. Every week when I got in the car to drive to campus, I felt as though I could take a deep breath. This was my time to focus not only on my education, but also on becoming the person I strived to be. Some might see this as strange and wonder how I could possibly feel a sense of calm by going to school, but going to school is like going home for me. I feel safe, welcome, respected, and valued. In class, I am truly free to be the educator and academic I am at my core.

The amount of learning that has taken place in this process so far has surpassed any other learning I have ever engaged in. I have been transformed. At the beginning of the program, a professor of mine spoke of the circle of what we don't know. He explained that the more we learn and know, the more we realize what we don't know. This rang so true for me because as I work towards completing my doctorate, I know there is so much more I need to learn, and I still have the hunger for it. I will never be done learning.

Where will the future lead me? The truth is, I'm not sure. One of my main goals in life is to make the greatest difference in as many lives as possible. Does that mean that someday I may be a principal, assistant superintendent, working for the Bill and Melinda Gates Foundation, or a congresswoman fighting for education? Maybe. But what I know for sure is that for now, I am right where I need to be.

Throughout this journey, I have learned and accomplished more than I ever thought possible. During this process, I have been able to explore the depths of my own abilities and have been transformed as I have learned to trust in new and worthwhile ways. Larger than the Dr. prefix in front of my name, this experience has let me unite essential components of my being, my career as a professional, as a student, and most importantly as a person. Most of all, I am different because I have always lived to learn, but through the journey of being a doctoral student, I have also learned to live.

CHAPTER 5

DIFFICULT CHOICES, SIMPLE DECISIONS

Keith Cunningham

It is safe to say that the path I traversed to reach my PhD hardly went according to some strategically laid out plan. It would be more correct to say I rather backed into the endeavor after several years dabbling in this or that before discovering it was something I wanted to pursue. Over the course of these wanderings I was never much concerned with niceties like careers, making money, or even worrying too much about what the future held exactly. Perhaps I even adhered to this mindset to a fault as there have been plenty of instances over the years when finances were ludicrously tight. However, I have always operated under the premise that if lack of money was my biggest problem, I really didn't have much of a problem at all, at least compared to much of the world that regularly gets by with less material wealth than we have in the United States. This thought was never too far from my consciousness at most times and I believe it has been key to my making it through schooling and life up to this point with my good humor intact.

Another important concept that has pulled me through has been my basic feelings about the general purpose of life. The only real long-term goal I can remember holding since my youngest days has been to somehow do my part to make the world a better place for my having been here. Naturally enough, this purpose has grown more nuanced and sophisticated as the years have gone by, but its basic

Beyond the Pride and the Privilege: The Stories of Doctoral Students and Work-Life Balance, pages 31–36.

premise has been the driving force making me who I am today and providing me with a bountiful supply of optimistic hope.

I eventually ended up becoming a high school teacher after an attempt to get a PhD in History and lose myself in the library was sidetracked by a brush with death and meeting my wonderful wife. While recovering from an illness and trying to support my newfound family, I accidentally discovered the great potential for doing widespread good by teaching. I thus ditched the monastic life of a historian and began my career in a public school in Central Texas. Having always been a naturally critical observer of my surroundings, it did not take long in this setting before I grew dismayed at what I saw as an inefficient, dysfunctional, and often inhumane public school system around me (and of which I was now a cog). If the system was not completely broke, it was far from performing the noble task I believed it should have been striving for, the one Dewey wrote of one hundred years ago.

Combining this sense of near outrage (I can get pretty passionate about these sorts of things) with a simple enjoyment of going to school (I would stay in college my entire life if possible), I began my doctorate in education in order to both gain knowledge of why the system worked liked it did and what I could do to help nudge it in a more efficient and humane direction. I also figured having those letters at the end of my name would provide me more of a platform to affect positive change, whether through entrance to the world of academia and the space to conduct critical research or train teachers in a more humanitarian pedagogy. At the very least it would open up opportunities for me to get my ideas out there in the form of writings such as I am doing now. Rather than just being some crank (nothing against cranks, though) in a classroom growling about moronically designed standardized tests or arbitrary discipline policies that marginalize the poor, perhaps I could get to a place where my grousing might actually lead to tangible improvements. If nothing else, it would represent an attempt to do something about a situation I found frustrating, rather than just stewing about it in my own head. I might not ever change the world, but I knew I would sleep better at night if I were trying to do *something*. Some seven years later, as I sit with degree in hand and searching for jobs in academia, this basic premise drives me still.

Like a stream running concurrent with my teaching and doctoral responsibilities to form what felt like a rapidly flowing river, I also had a young family to occupy my attention. Seeing how my most natural inclination lies with spending the day goofing around with my children, there was absolutely no way I was going to let this whole newfangled career and PhD thing get in the way of my family relationships. They have always been my priority. I promised myself that I would never stray from this simple truth that is the foundation upon which I have built my past, present, and future. I had a professor tell me that the dissertation process would entail ignoring little fingers wiggling for my attention under the door while I dutifully kept writing, that during this time my wife would frequently feel like a single parent. Screw that. If it ever came to that point I would walk away. My time with my children and wife is beyond precious; believing steadfastly in the cliché that actions speak louder than words, if I ever found myself breaking this vow by spending more time with my doctorate than I did with my family I would walk away. I would not talk a big game about how being a father was the most important thing to me while I isolated myself within my studies.

The only solution to this problem seemed to be forgoing a couple hours of sleep per day. I was not too ecstatic at the prospect, but I figured it would only be for a relatively short time period and the sacrifice well worth the cost. This option seemed even more palatable after we hatched a plan wherein I would teach for a couple more years while my wife stayed at home with our children (we had also decided that one of us would always be at home with the kids, as long as we could afford to do so while keeping food on the table and a rood overhead). After that, I would quit to focus on my dissertation while she went back to work.

Unfortunately, this plan evaporated along with my wife's health as she developed spine problems and an autoimmune disease whose source and cure we are still trying to nail down with exactitude. The illness incapacitates her to a great extent a good chunk out of each week. When she is able to move around with relatively few limitations, if she exerts herself too much during these times she inevitably suffers debilitating pain in the days following. The chances of her getting a job and my staying home with the kids while finishing up my dissertation pretty much went out the window at this point.

To make matters even more difficult, my domestic responsibilities were also substantially increased now. Of course, I have always attempted to uphold my share of the burden in these matters simply because it is the right thing to do, especially given my staunch anti-misogynistic outlook; it also didn't hurt that I have long found cleaning and such to be rather cathartic. Suddenly, though, I had to shift from cleaning and cooking because it was enjoyable and equitable and face a new reality where I must take on the lion's share of these responsibilities because I had to.

So, instead of being able to focus on my dissertation as planned, I now found myself with considerably less time than before, which was saying a lot because I was already running close to empty in this department. Indeed, I had been rationing my sleep for years by this point. Now I had to do so even more because I remained determined this setback was not going to lead me to neglect my family or allow our house to slip into a state of disrepair, either of which I knew would only heap stress onto my wife. She was coming to grips with living with omnipresent pain and the potential for much greater disability in the future. I knew that dealing with an unkempt house or an absent husband would not be healthy for her as she grappled with this new reality.

I was therefore obliged to become even more disciplined, strategic, and efficient with how I delegated my time and effort. For instance, I began cooking all our meals for the week during the early weekend mornings while my family slept in order to free up time when I got home from work. I purposefully chose recipes such as stews or casseroles that allowed me to assemble the ingredients and then do something else while they cooked more or less on their own. I cleaned the main parts of the house in the evenings while the kids prepared for bed and attended to the smaller details as best I could whenever I found a free moment. If I needed a break from writing I would do something like clean part of the bathroom or throw a pot of beans on the stove, thereby accomplishing both a household task that needed to get done while breaking up the monotony of schoolwork.

After some careful consideration and trial and error, I established a loose schedule to more or less follow. I would wake up around 4:00 each morning (there were plenty of instances when I was unable to do this, admittedly) and do schoolwork until it was time to get ready for work at 7:00. This consistently gave me 2–3 hours of school time each day which was obviously crucial to my finishing. When I returned home in the late afternoon I purposefully (or did my best to do so) put away all distractions while I focused on the kids until they began to get ready for bed at 7:00. While they took baths and whatnot, I would hurriedly pick up the house for an hour or so, and then read them each a story before they went to sleep. Depending upon how late it was by this point I would either pass out myself (not uncommon) or catch a few quiet moments with my wife. I was pretty religious about getting to bed by 10:00 at the absolute latest so that I could be up at 4:00 the next morning and still receive a minimum six hours sleep. Any less seemed like it would jeopardize my health and I was determined not to go down that path.

On weekends and holidays we tended to stay up late playing games and such and then my family would subsequently sleep in the next morning, thereby permitting me a few more quiet hours to get work done. I would naturally sleep in past 4:00 on these days, but still usually managed to rise early enough to accomplish some writing or research.

I can admit now that I am finished—I consciously steered clear of such thoughts while I was plugging away like this, figuring that they would only serve to discourage me if I dwelt upon them—that it frequently felt like a never-ending task, but I am proud to say that I performed it to the best of my ability and still managed to spend just about as much time with my family as beforehand when I was "only" working as a full time teacher. Indeed, my wife has repeatedly expressed amazement at how little my studies seemed to impact her and our children's lives; she had certainly expected it to be much more intrusive.

For the most part I was able to accomplish this with very little stress, despite the fact that I was still teaching high school, carrying a load of 2–3 preps per semester with somewhere around 100 students. I attribute this mainly to my own attitude of stubbornly viewing life optimistically, the belief that I was achieving my goal of making a positive difference in the world via my interactions with students and the thrust of my research, and the omnipresent awareness that whatever I was dealing with there were undoubtedly millions elsewhere who would gladly change circumstances with me: I had a loving family, a tight circle of friends, and meaningful employment that enabled my to feed and shelter my family. I was fully cognizant that I could not reasonably ask for much more than this out of life.

This awareness was made all the more tangible by the nature of my dissertation (it is study of federal homeless education policy) and weekly volunteer work with kids at a homeless shelter. Not only was I thereby visibly reminded on a regular basis of how good I had it compared to many others, I was also driven to continue working to the best of my ability to hopefully put my knowledge and academic credentials to use to help fix a situation that is one of the shames of American society. I sincerely believe I have been blessed to find myself in a situation where, due to my insight, experience, and academic training, I am situated to make a positive difference on a larger scale that I ever imagined possible and this helped provide the drive I needed to keep digging away toward my goal.

I was constantly confronted with the troubling results of our society not treating each other as members of the larger community to which we all belong. How could I not be both righteously indignant and inspired by this? How could I not continue to do my small part to find a solution? How could I not feel lucky to be in a position where I could do something I love—go to school and explore ideas—and use the knowledge and credentials thereby earned to do something that holds such meaning for the way I intrinsically view the purpose of my life? To do otherwise would have been to see a human problem, be aware that I had something to contribute to its alleviation, and to turn away because it was difficult; this was simply not an option.

Of course, I would be lying to say that it did not sometimes seem overwhelming, especially when I saw my wife go through bouts of agony with no horizon in sight; sometimes the future implications of her illness frighten both of us to our core. There is no way to totally avoid this specter as it haunts so many aspects of our lives, from chemotherapy to frustrating physical limitations. It was also difficult being tired most of the time and near flat broke about three-quarters of it (teachers don't get paid too much in the first place and the cash we pay out each month for health care, even with insurance, is substantial).

I have also undoubtedly sacrificed some career prospects due to the choices I made while going to school. Obviously, networking and exposure to others are important to pursuing jobs in this field and I have knowingly forgone chances to foster these sorts of connections over the course of my doctorate. I only minimally participated in opportunities such as conferences and student organizations because doing so entailed giving up a weekend with my family here, or a couple of nights a month there. I was already stretched so thin with my time as it was that I could not justify being away more than was already necessary; I believe that too much of this sort of thing would have had a detrimental effect on my family's mental health.

As the opportunity cost for these decisions, I now stand with my degree in hand facing a more difficult prospect for landing a job in higher education than would likely have been if I had been more outgoing during these past few years. Indeed, my classmates who have already landed professor positions were typically very strategically involved with various conferences, professors, and organizations in order to facilitate the process of landing a job in academia. However, most of those that took this approach were younger and did not have young children. This changed everything.

Nevertheless, I have nothing to complain about. I made my choices and seized this opportunity on my own terms and according to my own timetable. And the rewards I got from it have been immense. I undoubtedly grew into a much more organized and systematic thinker as a result of my doctorate experience. I am clearly more proficient at expressing my thoughts to others in a more comprehensible and logic manner. It has made me a better teacher in the classroom and given me a more nuanced understanding of history and society. It has opened up new possibilities for me to make a more widespread difference in the world, whether it is through writing a journal article about how the educational system is not meeting the needs of homeless children or bringing a critical pedagogical perspective to a professorial position in a teacher education program somewhere. Indeed, I believe the process of earning my PhD has made me a better and more well-rounded person overall. Reflecting on the experience, as writing this has forced me to do in a very deliberate manner, it was undoubtedly well worth the effort, sleep deprivation and all.

CHAPTER 6

TYING LIFE TOGETHER

Taurean Davis

For me, the hardest part about my doctoral program isn't the amount of reading or writing that I do. Even narrowing my research focus to begin my dissertation isn't as hard for me. The hardest part is seeing a family member go through the worst moments of their life and you, alone, lack the ability to significantly help without sacrificing other things you also care about. Since enrolling into my doctoral program my life has been a unique balancing act. On one side I have my mother, who is very important to me. On the other side I have my academic priorities and career aspirations. My life story doesn't allow me to drop either side, or even focus on one more than the other. Before I share with you how I try to maintain work-life balance within my doctoral program, I want you to understand how difficult keeping the balance can be by understanding my past.

EDUCATIONAL TIES

I was born and mostly raised in a small, rural town in South Carolina where seeing gardens or livestock was only a backyard away. My mother, my younger sister and I weren't rich by any means, but we lived together, laughed together, and grew together – rich experiences Momma calls them. These experiences were always educational even if they weren't intended to be. I learned so much from my

Beyond the Pride and the Privilege: The Stories of Doctoral Students and Work-Life Balance, pages 37–41.

childhood and my relationship with family that family experiences have shaped the way I view my life and service to others.

Education and how I was raised literally go hand in hand. My family has always tied life experience and educational experience together. The pursuit of knowledge and being a service to others were taught to me by my teachers in school and by my mother outside of school. Like me, my mother is passionate about education. She lived through integration and understood the possibilities that education could provide for a young Black man from South Carolina. I guess that's why going back to college to get my PhD is no surprise to anyone who knows my family and how I grew up. After giving birth to me during her sophomore year, my mother never finished college, but she instilled in her two children the importance of going beyond high school to learn.

So, I decided to go to college and to go even further in my educational career by completing my master's degree. I didn't feel pressured to honor my mother's wishes. My mother never pressured us to do anything we did not want to do. I actually love learning. Because my mother didn't have the opportunity to finish college, the idea of making her even more proud of me than she already is was a bonus. Specifically, I wanted to make the family proud by taking the experiences I've learned and seeing how far they could take me, or better yet, take us.

FAMILY TIES

My earliest memory is the sound of muffled crying. I remember waking up in the middle of the night and seeing a low light from under my bedroom door. I got myself out of the bed and walked towards the source of crying and light. I vividly remember my mother at our kitchen table with several pieces of paper and mail scattered about the tabletop. Among the pile were a large, yellow note pad and a small calculator. Her head was buried in her hands and I stood frozen at the sight. My mother was strong - the lioness type. To our family she was the hunter and the provider. Honestly, my mind couldn't comprehend what made her so sad, but I know I wanted to help.

It took me several years after that to understand why my mother was so sad that night. However, it did not take me long to realize we were not a rich family. Times were hard when I was young. Financially, my mother tried to do everything she could for us by taking care of our needs first, and, if possible, giving us a few wants along the way. As I think back, Christmas time was always fun as a child. I remember when I was little I would see a few toys under the tree Christmas morning and say aloud, "Is this all Santa left for me, Momma?" She would smile and say, "Noooo… Now, you know Santa likes to hide things around the house, right? So, there's no telling what Santa has around here that we might find tomorrow or even next week!" I would always get real excited when weeks later helping my mother sort through the laundry to a find a *Masters of the Universe: He-Man* action figure at the bottom of the basket. It makes me smile to remember that. My mother tried very hard to make sure we had whatever we needed and wanted. I didn't realize till later that my mother was Santa and that additional week allowed her to get another check from extra days at work. Aside from my need to push myself to learn more I wanted to make more money to provide for my family.

My mother is my best friend. I've never been afraid to say it. Sure, it wasn't necessarily the topic of discussion with friends when I was in middle school, but I've never been ashamed of the close relationship I have with my mother. When I was growing up I always felt my family was unique. My sister and I had the most active parent during our years in school. My mother worked three jobs to provide for us and still managed to be on every executive PTA board throughout my K-12 experience.

During the most confusing times of my life I've always sought help from my mother. Talking to my mother is sometimes better than talking to a counselor because she knows me so well. She knows my strengths and my weaknesses and never tells me what I should do, but instead helps me understand possible options and helps me find my answer without even knowing what she might think is best. I know politicians who aren't even that savvy.

From talking to my mother and reflecting on my past experiences I wanted to leave South Carolina and discover more about the world and myself after finishing my master's degree. I decided there was much more to explore and learn that South Carolina alone could not teach me. My mother always said limited exposure to the world could undoubtedly limit your understanding of what you can learn. I wanted to learn as much as possible and not just for her sake nor the opportunities she did not have, but for myself.

But, sadly I also felt a little guilty about leaving because my mother started having complications with her heart and a myriad of other health problems. While nothing related to her health was to the point where doctors were doubtful about her living a long and productive life, she could no longer work and her body ached with frequent and intense pain. I knew I couldn't change what was happening to my mother, but remember she is my best friend, too. No one likes to see a friend in pain. But, I also knew I needed to leave South Carolina for myself. My mother never told me to stay and never made me feel bad about my decision to leave. So, in 2008 I left South Carolina to work at a university in Virginia to begin my career in student affairs.

WORK AND LIFE TIES

After four years working in Virginia I decided to come back to South Carolina and apply to Clemson University's Educational Leadership program to continue my education with faculty I had previously worked with and respected, while giving me the opportunity to be closer to my family. I missed them dearly.

My mother had two leg amputations within a year. The second of these amputations happened when I moved back to South Carolina. I had several months to stay with her before classes started, so I hoped to help out my sister with taking care of the house and my mother as well as taking a load off my grandparents who also helped out when they could. During this process I looked to my sister for emotional support. She took care of things while I was in Virginia. Unfortunately, my sister did not understand why I had to start the doctoral program immediately after moving back to South Carolina with my mother's current health situation. "You are really going to start school, Taurean? Really?" The expression on her face almost made me ashamed of my decision. Was I really abandoning my family obligations by selfishly pursing other interests right now? Should I wait? How long did I have to wait before I could pursue my own interests?

My apartment is about 45 minutes from my mother's house. A typical week during the semester includes at least three journeys to my mother's house. Sometimes my mother has the occasional surgery or procedure that requires a great deal of my time for support. Sometimes I need to help my mother run errands for the day when she is well and at home. Other times, the emotional toll of losing both legs can make her very sad. I don't want her to be alone during times like these. She never left my sister or me during our lowest moments in life. But, even more than trying to make my mother feel better and help her, I love our conversations. We are able to talk more about life. Now that I am older than the child who once lived with mom, our conversations are about how to appreciate what life gives you. She always says that she never would have imagined she would end up in her condition. But she always concludes by saying life also gave her two beautiful children and that she would do it all over again if it meant my sister and I would have opportunities she did not have.

Now that I've started my doctoral program balancing all of my responsibilities as a student and part of a close knit family is still difficult to manage. Any given week my cohort discusses spending time together downtown to take a break from classes. "Taurean, are you planning on joining us this weekend? Wait, no, I know you are always busy." While I know my friends are only joking, I know that I am missing out on opportunities to bond with my fellow classmates. I don't feel as close to my cohort as other students might feel.

I am a full time student with a teaching assistantship that keeps me very busy. In my attempt to balance both my life priorities and my academic ones, I usually do not have as much time to dedicate to extra, outside of class research opportunities as other full time students. Additionally, going to conferences and workshops out of town requires me to notify my sister and grandparents to make sure my mother has other family members around just in case something goes wrong. There is a great deal of planning outside of my curriculum as there is inside a doctoral curriculum.

There are times I honestly have to choose between getting an early start on classwork and spending time with my mother. My first year in the doctoral program, I felt bad that I had to make these types of decisions when others did not. But, after reflecting upon my first year as a successful student I now know there are many students with obstacles that could easily detour others from finishing the degree. Not everyone has a doctoral degree or is as fortunate to say they are even pursuing one. I'm impressed with my balancing act thus far. I'm satisfying my need to pursue my interests, but I am remaining true to myself and my family by helping those I love the most.

The most important thing to realize before you decide to pursue a doctorate consider all of the possible influences in your life. Never forget that your wants and needs are also a major part of your life. Specifically, be comfortable with yourself because in times of uncertainty it is your understanding of who you are that will get you through all the questioning that your mind will create to potentially stop your progress. I don't focus as much on what I don't have anymore. I am blessed to have family who loves me and a cohort who continues to support me outside of my family support. I'm not forced to be tied by anything life gives me. As I continue to tie together each string of my life priorities, I realize that the merger has made me a much more experienced student of school and life.

CHAPTER 7

TICK, TOCK-CLOCK

The Never Ending Clock

Chinasa A. Elue

4:30 am: My arm swings over to silence my alarm signaling the start of a new day. It's Monday morning and as I turn off the alarm, I can't help but wonder to myself, "Where has the weekend gone?" I left campus the previous Friday with goals to accomplish a mound of academic work over the weekend, only to be reminded this morning of how far I was from reaching those three day old goals. I quickly scurry up and reach for my bible on my lamp stand and have my daily devotion before I begin to prepare for my day. This sacred time reminds me to be thankful for the gift of life before embarking on the grueling day ahead of me.

5:30 am: I put on my gym clothes and quickly scurry out the door to my 6 am boot camp session at the campus gym. As I return back, I heat up my bowl of oatmeal and watch the early morning news before heading on to campus. This time is cathartic to me as I am gearing up mentally for the day.

10:00 am: I make my way to campus to my graduate assistantship and prepare for the long day ahead. Between meetings with committees, students, and advisors, I know that the week will be packed. But hey, this is my life now as a doctoral student. As I rise each morning, I am baffled at the highway long to-do list I have on my desk and wonder how on earth I will get everything done. I don't

Beyond the Pride and the Privilege: The Stories of Doctoral Students and Work-Life Balance, pages 43–47.

know how I make it, but I always do. Before I take you more into my journey, let me share with you how I reached this critical juncture in my educational career.

GROWING UP IN THE ROCK

I am a Georgia Peach. Growing up in good ole' Stone Mountain, GA, I enjoyed everything the South had to offer, from home-style southern cooking to watching the laser shows at the nearby Stone Mountain Park. My parents matriculated to the United States from Nigeria to pursue higher education and instilled in me and my siblings at an early age the importance of an education. Growing up in our household was like growing up in two worlds- one where you had your cultural roots and ate Nigerian delicacies such as foo foo and Jellof rice, but also went to school and ate hotdogs and pizza like it was the best thing since sliced bread. In my parents' eyes, not only was going to college not an option, but my major also seemed non-negotiable, hence my initial decision to pursue a degree in biology pre-med. In my parents eyes, this degree track would be the most honorable and lucrative, and being the first child of four children, I felt obliged to give in to their desires. I soon discovered that my dislike for needles and blood would win out over my desire for this degree (not to mention the coursework) and I decided to switch tracks. As I broke my parents' dreams by informing them that I would no longer be their medical doctor, I promised them that I would one day be a "doctor" of another kind. Hence, as I progressed in my academic career, I discovered my love for people and the field of education and opted instead to pursue a Master's degree in educational leadership and later my doctorate in the same field. I can honestly say it has truly been a journey. One that has been marked with several small victories and defeats, but I am always keeping my eye on the finish line.

AIN'T NOBODY GOT TIME FOR THAT

I am sister, daughter, friend, counselor, student, minister, all rolled up in one person. All of these roles demand some portion of my time; however, I often find myself echoing the words of the popular YouTube sensation Sweet Brown "ain't nobody got time for that". So in order to make time and balance I have had to adapt in order to survive and multitasking has become imperative. For example, I catch up with mom and friends between walking to my car or driving home. I clean my house once a week and I have resulted to cooking in mass production on Sundays to help with staying fit, saving time during the week, as well as money. Although my hometown is not too far from my institution, I have found that my trips down Interstate- 85 South have decreased to once a month. Even this one trip home a month is more times than my peers see their family in one year. Unfortunately, when I do arrive home for a weekend visit, I am often inundated with several tasks from church activities to finding time at a nearby coffee shop to get some writing time in. Thus, any type of family time even when I am in town is often dismal and strained. Nonetheless, I have been blessed with a father who pursued his doctoral degree and understands the daily rigor and grind that comes with the PhD process and a mother who provides me with several hugs just to let me know she cares and supports me. It is only during the winter holidays that I can slightly let my hair down and hang out with my siblings and parents even though my thoughts are constantly lingering on how I can use my time efficiently during the holidays to catch up on my writing and other tasks before the upcoming semester. I have found that this process of navigating how to allocate my time to get everything on my plate done is a daily struggle but one that constantly changes with the ebbs and flows of life.

THE DRIVING FORCE

My constant battles with time and my effort to balance my life have driven me to some unusual behaviors. I take literature with me everywhere I go for fear of wasting my time. I could be sitting in traffic, or in the waiting room to see the dentist and you can bet an article is tucked away in my purse for fear of not maximizing my time. This PhD process permeates every area of my life. I cannot and do NOT have the luxury of wasting a minute so I maximize my chances of being able to study or read wherever I am for fear of falling behind. School drives my life and I try to balance everything else around it—the stakes are too high at this level and time not spent working on research or my school work is time that I struggle releasing to any other task. As a result, I have become the queen of multitasking. If I can do two or more things at once, trust me when I say I will master it and master it well! Let me be honest and say that choosing to pursue a doctoral education full-time is a privilege. It is not mandatory that I do this at any costs, but it is a decision I have made to accomplish this goal; hence my decisions and my time saving tactics are all integral components for me to complete this process.

FROM MY LIFE TO YOURS

As I have gone through this journey, I realize there are several coping mechanisms that I have discovered that have been of great help to me with attempting to find a balance in my life. I can only offer some helpful tips that have been instrumental to me that may be helpful to others sharing a similar experience. I humbly offer these tips and hope that you are able to incorporate some of them into your daily endeavors.

1. Find your source of hope and go to it when you need support. For some that may be your faith, your family, or some other entity. For me, I found that my relationship with Jesus Christ provided me with hope when I felt the work load was too much, the time was too small, and the tasks at hand was too large. I would go to the source of my hope and find strength and encouragement to go on knowing that "this too shall pass". I have found myself growing more in my faith as a result of this process. I be-

lieve that if I could not turn to God during my darkest hour, that I would not have persisted through my program so far. It is "in Him I live, and move, and have my being (Acts 17:28). I simply find peace and comfort knowing that He will never leave me nor forsake me, so I trudge ahead, with determination knowing and believing that I will be victorious in this goal.

2. Go to bed! Just like the famous army slogan "Be all that you can be", I have found that I cannot be the best me as a doctoral student when I was stressed, sleep deprived, and malnourished. When I realized that sleep was an integral part to my existence as a doc student, I quickly adjusted my life to get at least 6–7 hours of sleep per night. The difference was tremendous! Now when I am reading articles, I am actually able to comprehend what I am reading instead of counting sheep on the inside of the pages. This revelation has allowed me to be more efficient with my time.
3. Health is Paramount. I would think to myself at times "I can't be tired, stressed, and fat! Oh heck no- something has got to give and it won't be my health!" Being physically active has been my saving grace as I have been trying to combat the stresses of life as a doctoral student. I have found in past semesters and times where I thought I would break down, that being active is a great form of therapy. A quick jog outside or a walk around campus did wonders for me physically and also served as a source of therapy. I have even been able to make losing weight a little fun by participating in weight loss challenges with my fellow graduate students. We have done various workouts together from taking kickboxing classes at a nearby gym to running in a few 5Ks together. This camaraderie has enabled us to support each other in our health goals while releasing stress.
4. Give me a break. Sometimes when I leave the office, I feel dissatisfied and downcast, for having the desires to take a break. The guilt that I feel at times for even taking the time to go see a movie after a grueling week weighs on my conscious but I have found that I have to adjust my expectations and goals of myself to enjoy this much deserved time and put the guilt on the backburner. Although these breaks do not happen often, I realize they are an integral part of helping me maintain balance. In times where I have forgone taking a much needed break, I have found myself often at the brink of a break down. Knowing oneself and your limits is important because you are able to set up some time for relaxation before you reach your breaking point. I am very aware of when I need rest and take time to relax when needed.
5. Mental Energy. A huge part of the doctoral process is writing. Finding time to write in the midst of all of the other tasks I have causes me grief, thus I have to find time to balance it into my schedule. I have found that writing when you have the most mental energy is important. I have dis-

covered that I am most active in the morning and in an effort to stop my writing anxiety of not writing at all, I try to maintain this critical time. I set my alarm to wake up in the morning and after my daily routine, I squeeze in my writing time even if it's just for 30 minutes to one hour. Although that time frame may be brief, I know by the end of the week I will have at least made progress in my writing. Incorporating this time is integral in helping me find balance between my schoolwork and personal life. If one area is off, it affects another area of my life.

REOCCURRING THOUGHTS

I have realized over the course of this process that work life balance is an ever evolving process- one to be quite frankly, I think is almost impossible to attain. When I give my all in my academics, I find that my physical appearance and upkeep lag behind. When I attempt to take a break, I find myself drifting into an abyss with all of the looming deadlines and work before me. Thus, I have come to the conclusion that there is never truly a balance. At the end of the semester I often sit and reflect with my friends on the "realness" of the semester. Somehow, I always manage to make it through the semester with all of my assignments turned in, my hair a little more greyed, and a little more hopeful that I am nearing the end of this process.

As I have embarked on this journey in graduate school, I have discovered time and time again that finding a balance honestly is a challenge. I can say through it all however, it has been a very rewarding experience but not without hard work and constant reflection on how to adjust and re-adjust my time to manage all of my many roles and responsibilities. I can only hope that as I transition beyond graduate school, that I will be able to learn from these experiences and use them to help me balance in my future roles.

CHAPTER 8

PIECING THE PUZZLE TOGETHER AND DECORATING OUR LIVES

Work-Life Balance and the Sacredness of Everyday Experiences

B. Genise Henry

I have always enjoyed the visual aesthetics of home décor. Whether it is painted walls filled with family photos or rich architectural design, the decorations in a home tell the stories of our lives. Growing up, the third child of four in a single-parent home, there was a limited amount of resources that would allow us to decorate. However, my mother was a puzzle enthusiast who spent her limited amount of free time piecing together jigsaw puzzles with nature scenes and other beautiful images. To appease my desire for home décor, my mother allowed me to use her completed puzzles to decorate the walls of our home. We glued together the backs of her completed puzzles to create homemade wall art. I noticed the most serene look in my mother's eyes when the puzzle glue dried and we would flip the puzzle over to look at it. She would rub her hand smoothly across the surface and smile before we found the best location to hang it somewhere around the house.

Beyond the Pride and the Privilege: The Stories of Doctoral Students and Work-Life Balance, pages 49–54.

Sometimes, after hanging the puzzle one of the pieces would end up coming off and somehow misplaced. She would then fuss about how the beauty of the puzzle was lost from that one missing piece.

I use this illustration to compare how all of the pieces of our lives are important when balancing work and life. In the first book on the series of work-life balance, *Juggling Flaming Chain Saws: Faculty in Educational Leadership Try to Balance Work and Family*, Marshall et al. (2012) described work-life balance as the tension between the demands of work and our lives outside of that work. Like the puzzle illustration, our lives are pieced together through the various roles and responsibilities that we have, which come together to decorate our lives. The roles and responsibilities that we maintain become the images we have for ourselves and the labels that we identify with.

DECORATED LIVES

I identify myself as an African American Christian woman, who is a wife, mother, daughter, sister, granddaughter, and friend. I am also an educator and life-long learner who is the first of my family, on both mine and my husband's side, to complete a doctoral degree. Since the recent completion of my doctorate, I am now often referred to as "docta" among some of my family and friends. When sharing my experience as a doctoral student and the other various roles that I maintained, I would often be met with awe and encouragement. However, I regretted sending the message that my work-life balance was intact, because what I did not share openly were my feelings of guilt from spending time away from my husband and children, the initial feelings of isolation from being a first generation doctoral student, other fears of underperformance at work due to the responsibilities of graduate study, and the emotional imbalance that was the result of my ongoing self-questioning about how the pursuit of a doctoral degree impacted my life in a holistic way. Rather than add guilty, fearful, isolated, and emotionally disturbed to my decorated life, I shamefully led others to believe that I was able to manageably handle and maintain everything with a good sense of balance and a smile.

The smile I wore kept others from prodding too deeply to discover anything more than what I intended for them to see and believe about my identity. hooks (2005) described this dissimulation as dysfunctional stating, "it encourages us to deny what we genuinely feel and experience [thus losing] our capacity to know who we really are and what we need and desire" (p. 15). This sort of dysfunction interrupted the progress and motivation along my path of doctoral work. As I reflect on my false contentment, I wish that I had come clean with myself and others sooner rather than later, recognizing that I could have used some help in understanding the intricacies of work-life balance as a doctoral student. If only I had expressed to someone the tensions that I faced between meeting all of the demands of work-life, perhaps I could have been offered some helpful advice that would have allowed me to remove the guilt, fear, isolation, and emotional anxiety that I allowed to weigh so heavily upon myself. Therefore, I offer this chapter as a reality check and confirmation to others with similarly decorated lives who may believe that their experiences are held in solitude, and who struggle to maintain work-life balance as a doctoral student.

MY REALITY CHECK

This journal entry (Figure 8.1) is an excerpt from my son's first grade journal that was written when I first entered the doctoral program. Unfortunately, it took me far too long to recognize how my decision to pursue a doctoral degree, while working full-time and maintaining a number of other responsibilities, painted an undesirable image of me to my children. While I appreciate teachers who allow children to journal about their experiences and thoughts on paper, the revealing words from the mouth of a babe are at times heart-wrenching. As Witherspoon

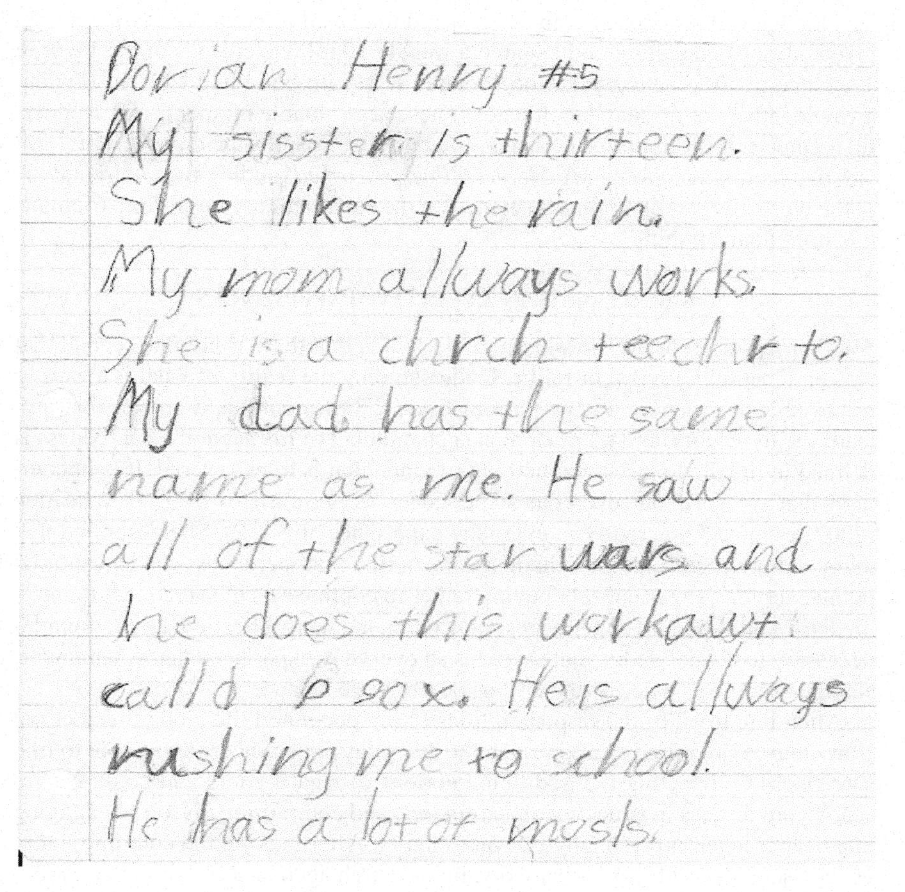
Dorian Henry #5
My sisster is thirteen.
She likes the rain.
My mom allways works.
She is a chrch teechr to.
My dad has the same
name as me. He saw
all of the star wars and
he does this workawt
calld p 90 x. He is allways
rushing me to school.
He has a lot of mosls.

FIGURE 8.1. My Son's First Grade Journal Entry

(2012) noted in her chapter of *Juggling flaming chain saws: Faculty in educational leadership try to balance work and family*, writing can not only help one be present in life, but reading about the experiences of others can help us reflect on our own. In this case, my first grader taught me something about myself. Reading my son's narrated interpretation of each of his family members allowed me to see that I needed to tip the scale of balance and show him that I could do more than "allways work." Recognizing that even a child's words can hold power to change lives, this was one example of the reality check that I needed to change mine.

Seeking to change my circumstances for the better, I began thinking about ways to creatively engage with my children while still accomplishing the work that I needed to do. My son and I began going to the library together on a weekly basis and then stopping for a frozen yogurt treat on the way home. This ritual became our sacred time. While we were able to share this time together, I was still able to accomplish my evening studying and writing. I also found other ways to develop habits that I considered to be sacred tokens of affection to share with my loved ones. My daughter and I shared a weekly 30 minute episode of her favorite T.V. sitcom while eating pizza on Monday's. My husband and I began stealing away together for midday lunch dates. These are valuable moments and wonderful memories that supported my work-life balance. Frankly, the thought of my son one day having the words *My Mother Allways Worked* (adding the additional "l" in the word always for emphasis) etched on the surface of my tombstone frightens me more than anything.

SACREDNESS IN EVERYDAY EXPERIENCES

Another lesson from my, now sixth grade son, is that there is not one second that we can recapture, revisit, or relive. Understanding the reality of what it means to not be able to recapture any part of our lives, as time continually moves forward, leads me to recognize that I must treat each moment of life sacredly. Sacredness is defined in the dictionary as something of value that is to be revered. It is uncommon that we view our everyday experiences as sacred. However, as Wheatley (2002) espoused "sacred is an everyday experience" (p. 132). She described that many cultures and traditions challenge the notion that sacredness can be captured in the everyday experience, believing rather to confine acts of sacredness to intermediaries and specific experiences. In accordance with Wheatley, I have found it necessary to acknowledge that sacred is an everyday experience that when understood can serve as a necessary vision for work-life balance.

Attending to all of the responsibilities of my decorated life along the doctoral study journey required sacredness in the everyday experiences. I was able to find sacredness by rejecting the traditional notions of what I could and could not research and discuss in educational institutions, and committing myself to engaging at a deeper level in personally relevant inquiry. After making the commitment to engage sacredly and whole-heartedly, my research agenda shifted from questioning the spiritual experiences of the educational school leader, to questioning how spirituality informed the experience and progress of doctoral students, including myself in the research. The decision to change my research, dissertation chair, and most of my committee delayed my progress towards completion, but it opened up a pathway for work-life balance that I could not see clearly at first. My writing became more than just words on a page, but sacred everyday experiences with intentions of the heart that allowed me to see how my work could impact others. Finally, immersed in research that I could relate to my friends, family, and to the educational system as a whole, I began to piece together the areas of my life that seemed disconnected. I could also see more clearly how the pursuit of a doctoral degree impacted my life in a holistic way, giving me the full conviction that I was doing work that mattered. This change in the way I viewed the everyday experiences of my life relieved me of much of the guilt that I had from my time away from family during study hours and the other feelings of inadequacy. Everything became intentional acts or, as described earlier, sacred tokens of affection. The transformation of my mind, in the way I viewed each moment of life as sacred, supported my ability to further balance life. This change allowed me to question life more thoroughly and to ultimately look at every aspect of my life to see where I was falling short of valuing it as sacred. In doing so, I discovered that the professional work that I was engaged in, which survived on the deception of others for the benefit of the organization, was not a place where I needed to be. Therefore, I resigned in order to find a position that would allow me to hold each moment as sacred. I was further able to piece my life together like the serene images of nature that my mother pieced together through her puzzles, therefore discovering the impact of work-life balance in every aspect of my life. Amends must be made in allowing sacredness in the everyday experience before change can happen. When I allowed myself to view every detail of my life in a sacred way, I changed my life for the balance.

FINISHING THE PUZZLE

Although my puzzle of work-life balance is still being pieced together, I have a vision of what the finished product will reveal. I see a large open area surrounded by trees where I am standing along with my family, friends, and colleagues, sharing in conversation. Unlike the historical view of the academic working on an esoteric project in a room filled with books, the changing demographics of modern academicians leads us to share learning in a different way and with a variety of people. My work-life balance rests in my ability to share my life in a holistic way with others. I hold on to the idea that my struggles to maintain work-life balance, when shared, may help someone else in their own struggle. Thus, I attend to the sacred everyday experiences, valuing each moment, and wholeheartedly engaging in life because I know that my work-life balance is dependent upon my recognition that after the glue dries the beauty of the puzzle can be lost in one missing piece.

REFERENCES

hooks, B. (2005). *Sisters of the yam: Black women and self-recovery.* Cambridge, MA: South End Press.

Marshall, J. M., Brooks, J. S., Brown, K. M., Bussey, L. H., Fusarelli, B., Gooden, M. A., Lugg, C. A. et al., (Eds.). (2012). *Juggling flaming chain saws: Faculty in educational leadership try to balance work and family.* Charlotte, NC: Information Age Publishing.

Wheatley, M. (2002). *Turning to one another.* San Francisco: Berrett-Koehler Publishers.

CHAPTER 9

DESEANDO TODO (DESIRING IT ALL)

Balancing Work and Life as a Latina in the Academy

Olga Martinez Hickman

> Mommy, when are you going to find time for me? You're always working or at school, it's like you have ten jobs.

Those are the piercing words my seven year old expressed to me exactly 43 days prior to my beginning a piece on balancing work and life. I marked the day on my calendar, took a picture, and set it as my screen saver as a reminder of how my life as a scholar affects those around me. As a wife and mother, I have aimed to find a balance between work and home. Growing up I saw *mami*—my own mother—leave home before the sun came up. I, like my own daughter, cried when she could not comb my hair on picture day, or when *papi* became angry with me when what he prepared for breakfast was not how *mami* would make it. Like my *mami*, I play many roles for many people.

Today, I have my own family, a career, aging parents, loved ones that are far away, friends, and then there is me. Every day I have a yesterday, but I also have a

Beyond the Pride and the Privilege: The Stories of Doctoral Students and Work-Life Balance, pages 55–60.

tomorrow. Daily, I aim to remember that I have the agency to be the author of my own book. I have chosen to follow a dream that I borrowed from other women. From them I learned the PhD was not impossible for me, a Latina who grew up on Monterreyito—a poverty-stricken neighborhood in South Texas. Along the way I realized that I was capable of pursuing my goal. However, I would have to find stability between work and home in order to satisfy all of the roles I play, and keep my sanity at the same time.

The equilibrium of work and home has often been situated as a challenge for women of color aspiring for the PhD (Castellanos, Gloria, Kaminumra, Vasquez, & Garza, 2006; Dowdy, 2008). Between personal, cultural, and institutional challenges, it is no wonder that scholars (Castellanos et al., 2006; Espino, Munoz, & Kiyama, 2010) aim to increase the number of Latinas in academia. Although the number of Latinos in higher education has risen dramatically in the last decade, with only a mere 3% of Latina/os earning a PhD in 2009, (National Center for Educational Statistics [NCES], 2012), the challenge of the Latina earning the advanced degree remains. As a Latina, I've dealt with negative stereotypes and assumptions my whole life. Pursuing a PhD has been no different. With staggering statistics coupled with cultural expectations, the process is difficult and often presents roadblocks to my own timeline. Very often, however, I must remember that there was more to me before I became a student.

There is no wealth but life.

— *John Ruskin*

Once upon a time, I was a wife, mother, daughter, sister, and friend. I had time to take trips, visit friends, make date nights, and even visit the gym daily. To the surprise of many, I continue to do the same today. Because even though I have many added responsibilities, I remind myself that this is a journey. I cannot cease to let myself exist.

When I made the decision to join the academy, I knew I would be juggling the demands of my personal life, career, and studies. Like others before me, upon beginning my journey into what seems like a part-time job, I found myself drowning in what Jyothi and Jyothi (2012) term *life balance conflicts*. I spent endless hours in front of a computer or sitting in a library, doing what I thought I should be doing to succeed through coursework. Every day, I began to spend less time with my husband, and missing out on important milestones. At the time, my daughter was three. While I thought it was cute for her to lie next to me to "do homework with mommy," I realized that I was no longer reading her childhood favorites. Instead, she was becoming quite the little qualitative researcher, as she listened to whatever I read out loud just to hear my voice.

Each day, I follow a routine that has been planned for weeks, even months. I choose to give myself the extra time that so many of us (women, scholars, professionals, and mothers) long for, and cannot find within our busy schedules. Long before the sun comes up, I am up. I have learned that if I am to enjoy all that life has to offer, I have to sacrifice a little of my sleep.

In 2009, I began my first semester as a doctoral student-as the wife of a high school varsity basketball coach, and a mother to a daughter and two dogs. Besides juggling my time, I also had to balance the family's finances. Not only was I a student, but my husband began working on his master's as well, and our daughter was attending private school. In essence, we were paying three tuition bills. Added to that, I worked for an institution that was over 300 miles away. For the past nine years, I have traveled monthly, sometimes weekly, to attend meetings or visit local schools. While it would have been nice to stay home, and be a full-time student, that was never an option.

> Real education should consist of drawing the goodness and the best out of our own students. What better books can there be than the books of humanity?
>
> — *Cesar Chavez (as cited in Castellano, et al., 2006)*

Latinas have confronted discrimination in and out of the academy and workforce, and have often been shunned by *nuestra jente*—our own people—for wanting to navigate unfamiliar territory (Castellanos et al., 2006). Although our community has often been criticized for having strict guidelines of what women can do, I am a firm believer that I have come to be who I am because of what I know, what I have experienced. It was those stringent rules that led me to stray and challenge tradition. Like other first-generation college students, I saw my parents do all they could so that I did not have to live the same poverty stricken life they did. When I was young, I felt that my working-class parents were invisible. They hardly ever attended any of my school functions and they trusted the teachers to show me the way of academia. In reality, they were preparing me for what Villenas and Morneo (2001) term *educación*- or education. Even though I was not even aware of it, they were guiding me as I learned to be humble and hardworking like them. By my parents doing this, I had the opportunity to navigate outside of the traditional role and the experiences of my parents, brothers, and sister, which I may have not been able to know.

From a father who left parochial school at 15 and a mother who never even completed elementary school, I learned the value of hard work and career attainment. Because of their struggles, I learned-the value of an education and bringing home a paycheck. Like Espino, Munoz and Kiyma (2010) explain, I know the smell of hard work by the memory of fresh cut grass, the smell of sweet tea, and my father's work shirt and boots. It took years of watching him walk home from work, his shirt drenched in sweat, to value a man who did all he knew to do to make sure his family would have enough. From my father I learned the value of a dollar, as I watched him balance his weekly paycheck on a napkin or small piece of paper he kept in his wallet (till this day he does not have a checkbook), to make sure all the bills were paid. From my mother, I learned the value of family. The sacrifice she made to leave us every day, to help my father maintain the home, taught me to do the same. While their value for my education may have been discounted by traditional terms, it was from them—my parents as my first teachers that I learned to become an equal contributor to our household. From them, I learned to weave what Delgado-Bernal (2008) calls the *trenza*-braid- of a combination of personal, professional, and shared identities weaved together. Through this *trenza,* I have been able to learn to make most pieces of my life fit together.

There were countless times when I left a newborn baby and husband behind to be on a plane one morning and in a class that same evening. The time I spent in cabs, planes, and hotel rooms became precious, although hard to swallow because I was away from home. It is there that I made time to read an article or study for class, in between Skype sessions or phone calls. Those moments in between important lunches and meetings have kept me from dinners with friends, or exploring a new city. Although exhausting, the time I spent away from home for work forced me to get things done while I was away, so that I could have time to spend with my family when I returned home. I found that every moment I spent away, I would never get back. Through my culture, *mi jente*-my people, and my parent's house on Holland Street, I learned that although I left behind part of my being when I joined the academy, I was still me. I still enjoyed late nights in the kitchen with family and friends, going to my parent's house just to see them, and taking trips with my sister, nieces, and nephews.

I continue to weave the *trenza,* wanting it to appear like a quilt whose seamless pieces of fabric come together to form a flawless piece. I know I hold the thread and needle, and my choices determine the final product. Parts of what holds me together are the pillars of support: my family, my friends, and my faith in God. My support system has come in many shapes and forms. My day begins and ends with family. I begin by preparing meals and wardrobes, and end it by reading stories, giving good night kisses, and catching up on the day's events. I have missed parent-teacher conferences, birthdays, and celebrations, but I have gained experiences, relationships, and knowledge that others may not have through my work in the academy. I acknowledge the fact that I may not follow the traditional role that society has designed for me, and I am at peace with this.

My husband, who is Black and not Latino, is not only another example of how I defied tradition, but also of endless support. He knows my story well, and has traveled a similar journey as a higher education scholar. As a graduate student himself, he recognized how precious time is. He has taken on the role some in society assumes belongs to the women, spending limitless hours with our daughter so that she does not see her mother as a slave to the books.

Together, we have accepted that every minute of my life matters, not for the here and now but for our future as well. In my role, as a wife, mother, and student, I refuse to take any of those moments for granted. I have also learned that a doctorate is not earned alone due to the many levels of support needed to achieve it. Finding the time to balance my work and home has seemed difficult at times, but I continue to do what women all over the world have done for centuries. I continue striving for what others have sometimes said is impossible. Each day, I understand and appreciate that I am a wife, a mother, a daughter, a sister, and a friend. I also look forward to tomorrow, adding the PhD. Certain expectations have been set upon me, not only as a woman, but also as a Latina and I continue to do what many others want to do; I write my own destiny. The same questions are asked of me quite often, "Why are you doing this? Haven't you been in school long enough? What about your family, who takes care of them?" My answer is not always shared with others, but I know exactly what it is. I do this because I want to, and because I can.

When I was a little girl, my sister combed my hair while our mother worked. As she tried to make the perfect braid with my thick, black hair, I sat on the hot living room floor and endured the discomfort of getting my hair tugged harder and harder. My *trenza*, today, consists of many strands. Like my sister, I have learned to pull harder so that it comes together almost perfectly.

A while back, my daughter asked a question that woke me up from the recurring routine I had become accustomed to. *Mommy, when are you going to find time for me?* Although she may not understand it yet, I do this for her. As a woman of color, I am setting a foundation, an example, and paving a road for her and others that come before, alongside, or after her. Although I cannot write the final chapters of her life, I can influence them. I choose to teach her indirectly, like my parents taught me. She sees me fill out three calendars, run from airports to classrooms, and rush home to get dinner ready. She also enjoys playing at the park, lying in bed together, and holding me in her arms. She has come to understand the balance in the midst of all the chaos.

I realize that what I am doing is not genius, it is not unique. However, in our home we value the choice of the PhD. We have learned that this experience has challenged the narrative that puts a limit on expectations for women of color. True, I am a student. And while the desire to follow this path was mine, my success is only made possible through the support I have received from my family. I do this for them. And while one day, I will be Dr. Olga Martinez Hickman, I will always be my Rejinah's mommy and Charles' wife.

REFERENCES

Castellanos, J., Gloria, A. M., Kaminmura, M., Vasquez, M., & Garza, H. (2006). *The Latina/o pathway to the PhD: Abriendo caminos*. Sterling, VA: Stylus.

Delgado-Bernal, D. (2008). La trenza de identidades: Weaving together my personal, professional and communal identities. In K. P. Gonzalez & R. V. Padilla (Eds.), *Doing the public good: Latina/o scholars engage civic participation.* Sterling, VA: Stylus Publishing, LLC.

Dowdy, J. (2008). *Phd stories: Conversations with my sisters*. Cresskill, N.J.: Hampton Press, Inc.

Espino, M. M., Munoz, S. M., & Kiyama, J. M. (2010). Transitioning from doctoral study to the academy: Theorizing trenzas of identity for Latina sister scholars. *Qualitative Inquiry, 16*(10), 804–818.

Jyothi, S. V., & Jvothi, P. (2012). Assessing work-life balance: From emotional intelligence and role efficacy of career women. *Advances in Management, 5*(6), 35–43.
Ruskin, J. (1986). *Unto this last and other writings.* London. England: Penguin Classics.
U.S. Department of Education, National Center for Education Statistics (2012). *The condition of education 2012.* Retrieved fromhttp://nces.edgov/fastfacts/display.asp?id=72
Villenas, S., & Moreno, M. (2001). To *valerse por si misma* between race, capitalism, and patriarchy: Latina mother-daughter pedagogies in North Carolina. *International Journal of Qualitative Studies in Education, 14*(5), 671–687.

CHAPTER 10

FINDING BALANCE BY AUTHORING YOUR OWN LIFE

Jennifer M. Horace

There is nothing more beautiful than seeing a person being themselves. Imagine going through your day being unapologetically you.
—Steve Maraboli (O'Brien, K., 2012).

It is very ironic that the month that I am writing this chapter is the month where I am in the midst of the most amount of stress I have experienced since starting graduate school. Balance does not describe my life. I am "juggling flaming chainsaws: (Marshall et al., 2012). My dissertation, job search, and personal life each need 100% percent of my attention; however, there is only one of me. During this time it is important for me to strive for balance in order to have peace and to do my work with excellence. To achieve personal and professional balance, I first acknowledge that all aspects of my identity are important and that sometimes they will conflict. Secondly, I must practice self-authorship. Self-authorship, the practice of making decisions based on my own priorities, has lead me to living a balanced and authentic life. In this chapter, I will discuss my identity, the meaning of self-authorship and how being my authentic self in the academe helps maintain work life balance.

Beyond the Pride and the Privilege: The Stories of Doctoral Students and Work-Life Balance, pages 61–66.

IDENTITY

Identity is a combination of an individual's unconscious mental model of themselves, their social contexts, and external forces that create a person's social identity (Jones, Kim, & Skendall, 2012). Because of the multiple forces that influence one's identity it is inevitable that aspects of our identities will overlap and conflict will occur. It is at these points of dissidence where we as graduate students question what our work-life balance should be. Questions such as how should we balance our lives as researchers, teachers, and students with our lives as members of families and communities. These lives are complicated by our memberships in social groups (i.e., race, gender, faith, sexual orientation, etc.). Each of these lives and identities comes with its' own expectations and pressures. Work-life balance is achieved through maturity (Komives, et al., 2007). Maturity comes from "knowing oneself well, building a personal life plan, learning to make good decisions, and acknowledging the capacity that one can learn and develop over time; in other words, it leads to being comfortable in your own skin" (Komives, et al., 2007, p. 388). This process is called self-authorship. Self authorship is how I maintain work-life balance.

For the purposes of this chapter I describe myself using the following labels: a doctoral candidate, an African American woman, a Christian, a member of a family, active member of a larger community, educator, scholar, research, student affairs practitioner, etc. Even while writing this list I thought of various ways to label the different parts of my identity or role I play in society. Each of my identities comes with its' own responsibilities in addition to expectations from others. At several points in my personal and professional life I received advice based on others expectations and opinions about what I should be doing with my life. It is in these life experiences where I realized that work life balance could not be achieved by living up to other expectations. I had to be the author of my own life; from this alone could come the peace that comes from work life balance.

OPINIONS FROM ALL DIRECTIONS

Throughout my life there has always been an abundance of people who have provided advice regarding my professional and personal life. While some of the advice was unsolicited, I believe that the counsel of others can be helpful because "[w]ithout good direction, people lose their way; the more wise counsel you follow, the better your chances" of success (Proverbs 11:14 The Message Version). But notice that it is "good direction" that leads to success. Every person who provides advice is not helpful. It is bad advice that results in unrealistic expectations of yourself and others' irrational assumptions about your abilities and time. Unrealistic expectations are what lead to an unbalanced life and increased stress. Therefore when listening to a person's advice it is important to 1) determine their level of expertise on the subject matter 2) their knowledge of you and 3) compare it to your values. We all receive advice but we retain power over our lives by electing what advice to implement and what information to disregard.

Wise Counsel or Poor Advice

I have received my share of counsel and I had to follow my own advice. For example, when I was preparing for my doctoral program one of my mentors/supervisors gave me a book that contained advice for African Americans interested in terminal degrees[1]. The book focused on all aspects of applying and completing doctoral programs. Most of the chapters were useful especially as I began to sift through my options of institutions and potential advisors. However as I progressed in the book, I began to question the necessity of some of the chapters as they began to focus on maintaining one's identity and not getting lost in the academy. I considered learning about these topics unnecessary given my professional experience and that my chosen doctoral institution would not be the first predominately White institution I attended. I was certain that losing myself was not going to happen but once I moved away from everything I knew to a small town in the south to pursue a PhD, I started receiving advice from all directions. People began to tell me what I should do in my professional and/or personal life. Advice came from faculty, administrators, family, friends in other programs, peers in my area of study, etc. They all meant well but their advice was faulty for one reason: they were providing advice considering one aspect of my identity as being far more important than any other. Some felt that I should be focusing on my identity as a researcher and focus my time on publications and presentations. While others thought I should be preparing to be a successful practitioner by staying involved in the student affairs procession. Yet another group thought it was a goodtime to set a foundation for a good personal life because I had already spent a large portion of my life focused on my career. To them it was time to focus on my family and starting my own. I quickly learned that these pieces of advice often turned into expectations. Having so many people place their diverse expectations on me lead to stress. Stress came from attempting to do too many things. Between classes, additional research projects, my assistantship, and personal life, my to do list grew longer and longer. Through this experience I found that it is important for me to practice self-authorship in order to ensure that throughout the journey towards the PhD that I was my authentic self.

SELF-AUTHORSHIP

Self-authorship is essential for graduate students "to meet typical expectations they face at work, home and school" (Baxter Magolda, 2008, p. 269) This will insure that they will be self motivated and guided by their own thoughts while balancing relationships with others (Baxter Magolda, 2008). The concept of self-authorship, developed by Robert Kegan, is supported by Baxter Magolda's (2008) twenty-one year longitudinal study of 18 to 39 year olds. Self-authorship requires that one develop an identity that will give them the confidence to act based on their own priorities (Komives, Lucas, & McMahon, 2007). Therefore being one's authentic self is the key to work life balance.

Self-authorship wasn't easy especially when I was a fulltime graduate student. Any doctoral student would agree because before you even start classes you are given a program of study or course manual outlining what classes you must take each semester, how long it will take us to complete the program, and even telling the times of the classes. Then you go to your job(s), whether it is a research or administrative, you are all pushed to meet the expectations of others based on others' ideas and possibly supporting their goals rather than our own. While we must succumb to those who have power over us in some cases there are opportunities for us to author our own lives.

As for me, and my struggle to maintain balance, I have had my successes and failures with this throughout my career. One way that I have been fortunate to consistently practice self-authorship is by controlling how I progress through my program of study. I extended my stay during each of my graduate student experiences. I stayed at a university as long as I was growing as a scholar or professionally. I didn't allow myself to be locked into the program plan or to be rushed to the next phase of my career. The majority of my publications and quality professional relationships came during that extra time I spent at each of my graduate programs. I am not saying that this is the correct thing for everyone to do but this form of self-authorship was right for me. Self-authorship is not easy but it was necessary for me to be balanced and at peace.

How to Practice Self-Authorship

Being one's authentic self happens by being true to one's character. It is about who you are, not what you do or what everyone is expecting you to be. When I started my journey towards my PhD, everyone had an opinion about what I should do but I had to stay true to myself. This is essential in preventing feelings of guilt and regret when not meeting other's expectations.

I encourage graduate students to reflect on what their life is about. What are your core values? For me, it is about creating positive social change. This inspires all that I am - researcher, teacher, student affairs practitioner, community volunteer, etc. Each of these aspects of my identity cannot be separated because they complement each other in order to insure that I am making a valuable contribution to society. For example, my dissertation research is grounded in the belief that it can help to improve an educational institution in my hometown. This perspective is in alignment with my core values and it helps me make decisions when aspects of my identity conflict. Despite having core principles that drives my work and life, sometimes conflict will still occur. When it happens I make a decision by critically considering my identity, social relations, and perspectives of others (Baxter Magolda, 2008). No matter what the result of the decision and whether it negatively affects my work or home life, I know that the decision was made by me, based on my core beliefs. When you practice self-authorship people will be disappointed but you can confidently ignore the naysayers because you know you will remain fundamentally true to yourself. People who are disappointed by your decision will let it go because they will see you growing to become an independent scholar and person. Ultimately, there is nothing more beautiful than seeing a person who is unapologetically themselves (O'Brien, K., 2012).

I will spend the rest of my chapter telling my story. I will try my best to be transparent in a manner that will help you find your own balance as a graduate student.

CONCLUDING THOUGHTS

As I conclude my narrative, I want to be honest and say that I know I am not perfect. All of my decisions have not resulted in great successes or major loses. But I know that I was able to balance others' expectations with my personal goals by being true to a set of principles that have helped me personally and professionally. I have talked about my commitment to doing work for positive social change but I am providing additional description of two of my principles with the hope those who read this will reflect on their lives and develop a similar list to help them make choices about their time and address issues when conflicts between their identities occur.

My Principles

My first principle is that my faith is important. As a result of this principle, there is always time for time at church and/or personal prayer and meditation. These things are built into my schedule like any other meeting, class or teaching assignment. This gives me a space where no one is talking to me as a researcher or educator. I have a place where no one asks about my latest study, conference, or publication. This time of pray and reflection gives me time to do a self-assessment of my values, who I am as a person, and where I am spending my time. It also helps me remember that I am a part of a larger society. This leads to my second principle: All of my skills, knowledge and abilities are used to help the larger society. As I peruse my curriculum vitae, all of my projects and positions that I have engaged as a researcher, practitioner and educator are ones where I believed that my skills were used to better society. Whether my dissertation research is about an institution in my hometown or teaching leadership theory to undergraduates, I do my work in a manner that will allow for me to better the community and to encourage others to do the same. Therefore, my research and teaching is about serving others. Sometimes, I am using my skills as a student other times it is as an educator or researcher. It is this perspective that helps me think bigger than me and my profession, my degree and my vitae. Maintaining balance can be difficult due to all the perspectives on how we spend our time. However "constructing a life for yourself is a dynamic process of self-assessment, reflection, and self-confidence in the context of your interest and relationship[s]" (Komives, et al., 2007, p. 388). As a graduate student, I have learned that practicing self-authorship in my life is important because it has helped me avoid professional and personal unhappiness. To my peers, determine what principles will help you make decisions in times of difficulty and this will help you find balance.

REFERENCES

Baxter Magolda, M. (2008). Three elements of self-authorship. *Journal of College Student Development, 49*(4), 269–284.

Jones, S. R., Kim, Y. C., & Skendall, K. C. (2012). (Re-)framing authenticity: Considering multiple social identities using autoethnographic and intersectional approaches. *The Journal of Higher Education. 83*(5), 698–723.

Komives, S. R., Lucas, N., & McMahon, T. R. (2007). *Exploring leadership: For college students who want to make a difference.* San Francisco, CA: John Wiley & Sons, Inc.

Marshall, J. M., Brooks, J. S., Brown, K. M., Bussey, L. H., Fusarelli, B., Gooden, M. A., Lugg, C, A., Reed, L. C., & Theoharis, G. (Eds.). (2012). *Juggling flaming chain saws: Academics in educational leadership try to balance work and family.* Charlotte, NC: Information Age Publishing.

O'Brien, K. (2012). *5 ways to become your authentic self today.* Huffington Post. Retrieved from http://www.huffingtonpost.com/2012/03/30/become-your-authentic-self_n_1392348.html

CHAPTER 11

MAINTAINING WORK-LIFE BALANCE AT THE CROSSROADS OF CULTURE

Éva Kardos

INTRODUCTION

I am a junior lecturer at the University of Debrecen in Hungary. I started working in this position in 2012 and I currently teach English descriptive grammar and theoretical linguistics in our undergraduate program. I now have the privilege to do what I have been dreaming about since I was a little girl. I can teach and think about English, which has been a favorite pastime and the love of my life since I was 10. My education has almost always revolved around this language. I attended a special English class in high school, studied English literature and linguistics as an undergraduate student, and then became a student of English linguistics in one of the graduate programs of linguistics at the University of Debrecen. Now that I have defended my doctoral dissertation, thus putting an end to my graduate studies, I have been looking for opportunities for self-reflection and this chapter appears to be an appropriate venue for that.

Graduate school in my case lasted six years, which I spent juggling between teaching, research, and family. In the meantime, I always had one particular goal

---

Beyond the Pride and the Privilege: The Stories of Doctoral Students and Work-Life Balance, pages 67–73.

in mind, my doctoral dissertation. These years have been the most fruitful and yet the most challenging years of my life so far. They involved lots of lessons learned and quite a few compromises. I almost always had multiple jobs, too many books to read and papers to write, and too little time to slow down and have some fun. The experiences that I gained over the course of these six years are quite varied because I spent about one fourth of this time in the United States, which is culturally very different from my home, Hungary, where I completed the rest of my graduate studies. Overall, I am happy about this period of my life. I now gladly share what I have learned hoping that this will help others who are about to start this "journey" or are already in it make the most of these years.

In what follows, I will concentrate on four issues that I believe are crucial in maintaining work-life balance. I address how having good problem-solving skills and confidence plays a role in achieving happiness and I also discuss the importance of a support system including supervisors, friends and family members, and a positive outlook on life.

The Study-Abroad Experiences

The fact that I was able to get an international perspective and multicultural experience helped me with a number of things, which all contributed to my living a more balanced and happy life while I was a graduate student. The study-abroad experiences provided me with a more open-minded attitude towards my work, and more importantly, they gave me the opportunity to improve my interpersonal skills and learn to truly appreciate the culturally diverse communities that I was temporally a member of.

As a graduate student I benefited from the five months that I spent at Indiana University in Bloomington and the eight months that I spent at the University of Texas at Austin as a Fulbright visiting student researcher. There are two aspects of these programs that I would like to highlight. First, I could gain insights into the life and work of local graduate students and faculty by attending classes, colloquia, workshops, and happy hours. Second, I also had the opportunity to collaborate with experts from different cultures and fields such as linguistics, education, and literary studies, and thus learn to look at problems from a multitude of viewpoints. These experiences have all shaped my thinking and ensured that I became a better problem-solver. This is certainly crucial for work-life balance in that this is what helps you increase your efficiency both in your work and personal life.

To be fair I must also mention that I have learned that doing graduate work abroad has its challenges, which can often negatively impact life on and off campus alike. For example, one of the initial difficulties that many international students face, I believe, is that we have to fit in with a new community and prove that we are capable of pursuing the kind of research that local students and faculty members are involved in. It can be quite a challenge since a visiting student may not have the background necessary for individual or collaborative work at his or her host institution. This can easily reveal itself in meetings with supervisors and in classes with fellow students. In my case the most awkward moments resulted from discussions with professors, especially at the beginning of my stay both in Bloomington and Austin. It became clear to me early on that I had serious gaps in my education and that I had no choice but to devote the first few months, oftentimes days and nights, to rigorous self-training and studying, which I often did in cafés and beautiful parks when I was in need of inspiration. At the time, I left very little room for fun and pleasure, but I hoped the hard work would pay off, and it did.

Another difficulty is that cultural differences can also negatively affect the efficiency of graduate work. For instance, lack of experience in interpersonal communication or the language barrier—which is always there to some extent regardless of how competent you are at a foreign language—can easily set one back, especially at the beginning of the study-abroad year or years. I also had these experiences. I have too many memories where I am with a group of American students and professors and I am surprised to see how confident and easy-going these people can be when they enter into a conversation and express their opinion. They seem to be at ease with friends, colleagues, and strangers alike, while I have a hard time saying a single word because, as a student from Eastern Europe, I am not used to such confidence and strong opinions. I also have countless memories where I am struggling to find the right word or sentence structure to say what I want, and since I am not successful in that, I feel inferior to the native speakers around me. This disadvantage in the English language also impacted my dissertation research. More specifically, given my limited experience in American rhetoric and writing, for instance, I always had to write several drafts of dissertation chapters before I eventually came up with a final version that was strong in tone and straightforward and convincing in terms of argumentation. This meant that, especially at the beginning of the writing process, I often spent hours constructing a single, paragraph-long argument by constantly rewriting my drafts. Similarly to the substantial gaps that I had in my field, my initial struggle with argumentation also resulted in considerably less time for life outside of work. And yet, despite this and other similar experiences, it is clear to me that if you have the eagerness to learn and a few close friends with whom you can share your positive and negative experiences, the advantages of such study-abroad programs supercede the disadvantages. After the initial hardships—and the feeling that you are inferior to others around you—you eventually start to fit in and make sense of the world around you. This in turn gives a sense of achievement and confidence, and you start to feel that you belong somewhere both in a personal and a professional sense. I was lucky enough to achieve this both in Indiana and Texas. As I started to understand the world around me, I began to feel at ease with professors and students alike and I actually started to enjoy my life immensely both in and outside of academia. This is what ensured that I could become more efficient in my work, which in turn helped me have a more balanced schedule, and after the first few months, avoid spending nights reading articles and writing dissertation chapters.

With all this behind me, I know that despite the initial difficulties I benefited greatly from these study-abroad experiences. I have become a more self-aware person, which is quite useful, albeit not sufficient, when it comes to such challenging tasks as conducting graduate-level research and having a life outside of academia. In what follows, I discuss what other aspects of the graduate school years ensured that I could achieve this.

The Importance of a Good Mentor

The most important goal in graduate school is the completion of the doctoral dissertation. This is quite a difficult task since you have to create something original that you can defend in front of scholars who generally have a very good understanding of your field. What you need to succeed in this is not only a solid foundation in the subject matter of your thesis, but also confidence and faith in what you are working on. The former (i.e. expertise in your field) is necessary so that you can produce a reasonably good thesis, while the latter (i.e. faith in your work) is what gives you the extra push you need to produce something that is a little better than good and this is what helps you keep sanity and motivation all through the dissertation project.

This project was quite a challenge in my case as well. There were two reasons for this: (1) I always had to work under time-pressure so that I could meet the various deadlines that my dissertation project involved; and (2) the problems that I addressed in my thesis were far from being trivial, which is something that, I assume, everyone working on a dissertation has to cope with. I often felt that providing adequate solutions to at least some of these problems was close to impossible given the multifaceted nature of my research and that I was a novice in my field. And this is where the need arises for a supportive advisor, who guides you through various parts of your analysis, pushes you to make the most of your work and encourages you to believe in yourself and stay confident. This guidance is essential so that one can maintain balance throughout the dissertation work.

I was lucky to have two advisors, who both ended up being important mentors to me. Interestingly enough, although they are from different countries, the United States and Hungary, they turned out to be very similar in terms of their thinking and personality: they would often ask the same questions, suggest the same examples to illustrate a given phenomenon, and they would even tell the same jokes! And yet they served somewhat different roles in my dissertation project. My American advisor was the one who instilled in me much curiosity and passion in the issues that I had to examine. I started working with him only about two years before my defense and I can honestly say that I would not have been able to submit my thesis without his encouragement, and most importantly, the enthusiasm that he always showed for the questions that I had to think about. On the other hand, my collaboration with my Hungarian advisor was a little different, but just as fruitful. He was the one who made sure that I stayed grounded during the rough times and the good times alike. He always asked me the most difficult questions, to which he always wanted the best answers, and he taught me to handle criticism and failure. He did all this in a way that I never once questioned that he wanted me to make progress and eventually succeed in my goal. Overall, it is without any doubt that these two people contributed significantly to my being able to achieve balance in graduate school by providing me with constant support, invaluable and often very exciting feedback, and guidance.

Looking back at the past six years, I am now confident that having such mentors is probably just as important as being part of a vibrant professional community and having a supportive family and friends. Next, I focus on how the latter two affected my life while I was a graduate student.

Professional Networking and Family Relationships

In my opinion, the building of professional and personal relationships are equally important if you aim to maintain a balanced life while you are in graduate school. As for the former, it is clear that you need a work environment that is conducive to creativity and productivity. On the one hand, the university that you are affiliated with is ideal for that since you are surrounded by numerous people who are interested in the same (or very similar) problems that you would like to figure out at various stages of your research. On the other hand, you can benefit greatly from the broader community that you are a member of since you can attend conferences, workshops, and other professional events, where you can put your thoughts to work or come up with new ideas. These experiences all contribute to becoming more aware of what your research goals should be and how it is best to achieve those goals in the most optimal way possible.

At the beginning of graduate school, I made sure to participate in a number of student conferences and workshops. At the time my objective was not so much to find specific answers to specific questions, but to get a sense of what others are doing and what problems are out there that I can approach with much interest and confidence. These events motivated me to want to achieve more and do something really useful and interesting. This, I think, is critical for good work and a positive attitude regardless of the field you pursue. If you are motivated and convinced that what you are doing has an added value of contributing to a better understanding of some problem in your field, you have a better chance of eventually achieving harmony in your personal and professional life.

A different but very important role is played by family and friends. Luckily, I met a lot of wonderful people during these six years both in Hungary and abroad. They always helped me feel good about and proud of my research and they also made sure to remind me of life outside of academia. I have countless memories of dinner parties that I hosted to sometimes very culturally diverse friends and family members. I also remember numerous day trips with fellow students and colleagues, or just friendly conversations over coffee and cake somewhere on campus. I cherished these events because they helped me relax and get away from the piles of books and chapter drafts on my desk. They also ensured that I could find a common ground with others and place myself in the community that I was part of. I often woke up very early in the morning so that I could fit these programs into my daily schedule because I knew it was often my friends who gave me the strength and inspiration that I needed to stay positive and carry on with my work.

Overall, then, the lesson I have learned from all this is that while networking with like-minded students and professors shapes your thinking, your family and friends keep things in perspective. They are the ones who are there for you when you fail in something and who encourage you to stay positive. These experiences are what I discuss next, in the final part of this chapter.

The Role of Failure and the Importance of Optimism

Having a positive outlook on life is probably the most important thing that will get you through the quite stressful years of graduate school. Moments when you feel you should give up on your professional goals that you have been nurturing for a while and start something new outside of academia may come in abundance at various stages of your graduate school experience: after an unsuccessful application for a fellowship that is crucial for your research, before qualifying exams; after harsh criticism on a paper, which begs the question whether you will ever belong to the research community in your field; and even close to the end, when you anxiously try to keep the deadline for the submission of your dissertation. Fortunately, however, many of us can get through the stressful times with a positive attitude and the ability to consider failure as an opportunity to learn and improve.

I personally always tried to make sure to set manageable goals and reward myself after I had completed an important project. This often meant that I attended friendly get-togethers, I went on short trips in Hungary and abroad, or I just bought a book by an author that I really like. I, of course, have not been successful at everything that I have tried. For example, I applied for the Fulbright scholarship twice and I got it only the second time in spite of the enormous amount of work I had put into my application. I also remember how the initial comments of my advisors on the first draft of my dissertation made me question everything I had worked for up to that point. They instilled in me doubts about my abilities regarding the work I was doing and undermined my confidence, at least temporarily. And yet I now strongly believe that these and other setbacks all contributed to the ultimate success of my graduate school years and the fact that I was able to maintain a balanced state of mind. They all taught me important lessons about how to address problems. In particular, I have learned that difficulties are in most cases not signs of one's incompetence, but they are there for us to understand and benefit from; they are inevitable landmarks for us so that we can grow both in our personal and professional lives.

In summary, I am happy about my decision to become a graduate student. Over the course of these six years, I improved my problem-solving skills, learned how to work more efficiently and manage my time wisely, and most importantly, I became a more confident person and learned to handle criticism and benefit from it. In my experience, these skills are crucial for anyone who would like to maintain balance in life. Also, I now have a clearer perspective of my professional and personal self and I am just more aware of what is necessary to have a happy life. Of course, I still have numerous goals to reach. One of these still concerns the question of how to maintain work-life balance. This time, however, now that I have started building a career in academia, I feel that the challenge to achieve this is greater than ever before.[1]

CHAPTER 12

LATE NIGHT PILLOW TALK

A Couple's Reflections on Balancing Marriage, Parenthood, and PhDs

Daniel Lipe and Kaiwipuni Lipe

Time Stamp: April 2013

Aloha and Osiyo! My name is Daniel "Bubba" Lipe and I am married to Kaiwipuni "Punihei" Lipe. I am Western-band Cherokee and grew up hunting in the woods and fishing along the rivers of Oregon. Punihei is Native Hawaiian and grew up on the island of O'ahu dancing hula and immersed in her language and culture. I moved to Hawai'i in 2005 when we got married. We now have two amazing children. Hā'ena Echota is our five-year-old daughter and Lamakū Noquisi is our two-year-old son. I defended my dissertation in February 2013 and officially graduate in May 2013 with a PhD in Education. During my six-year doctoral journey, I was a part-time student and worked full-time, first as a charter school teacher and then as an educational specialist at the University of Hawai'i at Mānoa. Punihei is ABD, having defended her comprehensive exams in October 2012. She is currently finishing data analysis for her dissertation in the College of Education and is scheduled to defend in May 2014. She is a full-time student and a graduate research assistant at the University of Hawai'i at Mānoa. Since begin-

Beyond the Pride and the Privilege: The Stories of Doctoral Students and Work-Life Balance, pages 75–82.

ning her doctoral program she took care of her elderly grandmother and is also the full-time caretaker for our son.

In order to shed light on some of the challenges and "survival" strategies that we have engaged, a dialogue between the two of us is shared below. We use this form of storytelling to highlight one of our strengths as a couple, the commitment to communicate, which has been foundational in our success and balance both at home and at school.

SETTING

Today Bubba turned in his final paperwork for his PhD graduation. It is now 10:30 p.m. at night. Our children are asleep. The floor has been swept but not all the dishes washed because in our single room studio, washing the remaining dishes will surely wake up the children. So after a long day, Bubba at his full-time job, and Punihei running after Lamakū, picking up Hā'ena from school, and working during their nap times, mommy and daddy are exhausted. Nevertheless, they are both extremely happy. Bubba is finally finished with school! So fighting to keep their eyes open, they lie next to each other and share in a little late night pillow talk, reflecting on the past, managing the present, and strategizing for the future.

Dialogue

Punihei: I'm proud of you. You did it! You must feel good, right? Relieved?

Bubba: It really hasn't set in yet. I'm actually not sure how to act now that I don't have to get up early tomorrow morning and write or even think about writing. It has been a long haul. At times I felt like I would never get to this point. It certainly has been one of the most stressful times in my life. It feels like a ton of bricks was taken off my chest today when I turned in my final paper. I feel exhausted yet totally relaxed. When I think back it seems so long ago that I cannot remember when it all started. Balancing my full-time job, family life, and trying to accomplish my work has been exhausting.

Punihei: I know. It has been exhausting. We are both *crazy* for doing this!

Bubba: I couldn't have accomplished this without your help. Without your organizational and editing skills I would still be writing my introduction. I think one of the most difficult things that I had to learn to balance was how to manage my stress of feeling like there was so much to get finished and feeling like it was going to be impossible. You really helped me to focus on one piece at a time. Another challenge was I kept finding different articles on topics I wanted to include. I think one of the best pieces of advice I ever received was from Margie [Dissertation Chair] was when she told me to stop reading and get busy writing!

Punihei: I clearly remember all of this. The main thing is that you're finished now. We both know that you could've given up a long time ago. We both know so many people who do. But you stuck to it. Now you need to go find your dream job!

Bubba: I also need to get back home to thank my mentors [also research participants]. I can't wait to see them face to face again. They really helped me from start to finish. Living here in Hawai'i has been extremely hard, as you know, especially when I think about not being around those folks for the last seven years. I miss them on so many levels. I miss just talking with them about hunting and fishing. I miss actually going out to hunt and fish with them. And during my dissertation research and writing, I felt terrible not meeting face to face with them.

Punihei: I know I don't know exactly how you feel because I'm not in your situation. I can see my mentors, my family, and my birth land almost on a daily basis. But I love you and when you are hurting, I hurt with you. That's why I was so happy when we took our family to see Tom [mentor and participant] last year in British Columbia. I could tell how much that meant to you. I think it was a much needed spiritual re-boost to give you some balance. I think it really was important for our whole family, actually.

Bubba: Yeah, you are totally right. I was feeling pretty beat up around the time we went to see him. I didn't realize just how much I depended upon them for support and mentoring until I moved here to Hawai'i. Even with these issues I am not sure I could have accomplished what I did without having the support of my mentors. Having a familial relationship between my family and my mentors and their families definitely helped me maintain balance and complete my dissertation. Even when I was only speaking to them on Skype, I really looked forward to that time to especially share family stories and what had been going on since the last time we spoke. We have both been very blessed to be able to work with such strong mentors who provide a shoulder to lean on and on other occasions a swift kick in the pants to keep us focused.

Punihei: Yup. You are absolutely right. We do have great mentors. And I want to make them proud by graduating soon. Like you said, I feel a huge sense of kuleana to my research topic, to my mentors, to you and our children, and to all the future people we want to support in education to do a good job with this dissertation and graduate soon! You know, so many folks define kuleana as responsibility, but it isn't just that. It is accountability and privilege as well. And I'm feeling it big time! Just like your work, this dissertation is not just a paper; it is a lifetime commitment and lifestyle. Which reminds me...I don't think I can do that book chapter on balancing life with graduate school.

Bubba: Why?

Punihei: I just have way too much stuff to do and the turnaround is too quick. I still have to finish my speech for my Montana trip next week and I'm still going through the transcripts from my interviews to prepare for my focus group. And Lamakū is down to only one nap a day. I'm feeling really overwhelmed again. If you want to do the chapter then you should do it on your own. Besides, you have a better success story than me. You're graduating. I haven't yet.

Bubba: But you are a part of my story and you also have your own story to share. I think we have a really important story to tell together. Two PhD students and two small children.

Punihei: Yes, but I don't feel like there's any balance to tell about. I feel like we are just in survival mode. I'm barely getting things done.

Bubba: Yes, but you still are getting them done. And we are still surviving! Seriously, you use every spare moment you have to do work. It's a little irritating, because I know it stresses you out. You really need to remember to take some time to rest, refocus, and re-energize. You are a workaholic, totally opposite from me. I remember you nagging at me to go write and I know I fought you but in the end I realized that you were really helping me the best way you could. You were helping me keep my momentum moving forward no matter how slow that momentum was. So remember that I am helping you the best way I know how by telling you to take a break. That is one of the best things about us. We tend to be on the opposite sides of the way we look at life. You are a typical type A personality. You are always stressed out about schedules and time. I tend to be more of a type B personality that goes with the flow. The great thing about us is that we can see when the other is going too far in one direction. So dear, what are you stressed out about?

Punihei: I just don't have enough time in the day to get things done. It was so much easier when Lamakū was little. I remember when I was still taking care of my grandma when he was just a baby and he would sleep for hours. I could get so much done. But once he started moving around everything changed. At first I still tried to do my work while he was awake. That's when I started using the baby gates to make a safe space for him to play. But he was so strong. He'd stand up, climb up on the gates, and then I'd end up chasing him around. So then I couldn't get my work done. I remember one day, Lamakū must have been about six months old, and I just started crying. I was feeling so overwhelmed by the work I had to do and not being able to get it all done. But I felt worse because I was getting frustrated with Lamakū for just being a baby and doing the normal things a baby is supposed to do. And I remember thinking to myself, what the hell am I doing? The whole point of choosing to stay home with him is so that I can be a good mom and provide a nurturing, fun, safe environment for him to grow up in. That's when I stopped doing work while he was awake. My new rule was, play with him while he is awake, and work when he is asleep.

It was about prioritizing. When I made that decision to stop working when Lamakū was awake, one of the things that kept going through my head was the lesson we had during my master's program in counseling about being present. So when Lamakū was awake but I was trying to also do my work, I realized that I wasn't being present with my own son! I felt terrible! But it was hard.

The other thing that makes me want to be a better mom even while working on my PhD is watching you with the children. You are always present with them, playing, teaching them how to do things, and cooking with them. You've been a good reminder to me about the kind of parent I want to be. The only thing that drives me crazy is that you fall asleep with them instead of doing your work.

Bubba: Hey! I finished my PhD. What more do you want?

Punihei: Yes, finally! But when you were working on your dissertation, I just couldn't believe that you would sleep instead of staying up to write. In my mind, when the children nap that's the time to get your work done.

Bubba: You're probably right. There's times when I should have stayed awake and wrote. But other times I knew I had to nap or I'd be sick or get a headache. I listen to my body!

Punihei: Hey! What are you trying to say?

Bubba: You know exactly what I'm trying to say, dear. It took you having a stroke at 28 years old to figure out that you had to listen to your body.

Punihei: Hey! Nobody can prove that I had that stroke because of lack of sleep! And it was just a *little* stroke. But you're right, that time in the hospital changed my life. But you've got to remember, I had stopped doing most of my work in the daytime because I was trying to be a good mom so I had to stay up late at night to finish things. When else was I supposed to do it?

Bubba: I don't know, but you've made it work so far. Just remember it is my job to support you and make sure that you are taking care of yourself. I remember walking down that hallway in the hospital holding Lamakū, walking past rooms where the youngest people in there were older than my grandparents and thinking, what in the hell are we doing here? I am glad that you have slowed down a little bit. Don't think for a minute that I will let you go back to that craziness.

Punihei: I know, when I was in the hospital, I had a conversation with Aukahi [friend] that really helped give me some perspective. I was explaining to her that the reason I was working so much at night was because I had this timeline that I *needed* to adhere to. So she asked me whose timeline that was. I told her that it was mine. Then she asked me what would happen if I moved things back a little bit, taking a few more months to write my dissertation proposal and prepare for my comprehensive exams. And honestly, I couldn't think of one big problem that I would run into. I was stressing myself out over the deadlines I had created for myself, but it actually was okay for me to move them. I had never thought about that before! Having the stroke was so terrifying that it didn't seem like such a big deal to push a few deadlines back if it meant I could be around to raise my children and grow old with you.

Bubba: What do you mean that was the first time you ever heard someone say don't worry too much about sticking to a timeline? That is my motto! It makes me think about going home to see my family and going hunting or fishing during my dissertation writing. Before moving to Hawai'i I was in the woods or on the river every day. When I moved here that all changed. Now when I go home I try to use that time away to find balance in myself. I know a lot of people didn't get it when I said I was going home to reconnect during my dissertation writing. They didn't understand that I needed that time for myself to find balance or else I would have lost my mind. I know you understand this and that is one of the many things I love about you. That is also why I am glad that you started going back to hula. It allows you a chance to refocus, to clear your mind and see things from a better place. If anything can help you find the balance you need to succeed it is doing something that makes you happy. Having some time to refocus and recharge in the forests that I grew up in is that connection for me. Besides, some of the best ideas I wrote about came from spending time in those places and making connections to the environments back home.

Punihei: I know. That's why, even though it is really difficult when you are gone for two weeks during hunting season, I always want you to go home. I know you need to smell the forest, walk in the woods with your family, and just be home. I know that you come back re-charged. I feel that way when I go to hula, too. Even though hula is only once a week for two hours, I seriously feel so much better after I dance. Just being around my hula sisters and kumu [teacher] is a huge re-energizer. And at every practice I learn or am reminded of something from my ancestors that really helps me with every other part of my life.

Bubba: That's totally foundational. It also helps make us who we are. Being in the woods removed all of the stresses of having to accomplish my dissertation. Without my trips to the woods I would have never made it. I am constantly telling my students the same thing: They need to find that "something" that allows them to re-energize, re-focus, and re-connect.

Punihei: Yes, you're right. We each need to find our own spiritual place. Also being home with Lamakū and thinking about his future, and being involved at Hāʻena's school, also push me to want to graduate. I know that having a PhD will open more doors for us to engage in the work we want and need to do in education for the sake of our children.

Bubba: I hope you reconsider doing the chapter on graduate student balance. I think we have a lot to share with people, students and families, who are going through the process of trying to earn their PhD while maintaining a sense of sanity. I think our stories could help them see that they are not alone, that others like us have struggled as well.

Punihei: I guess you're right. There are the big things like supporting each other and remembering our spiritual connections that are helpful, but there are also the small things that I think are really important too, like working during nap times, taking turns for an hour to go hide and write while the other parent watches the children. Or even remember when I would leave you home to write and I would take the children to the birthday parties, the graduation parties, or whatever other kind of engagement our family needed to attend? Making time out of seemingly

	no time, but all because we have a commitment to both of us graduating!
Bubba:	You're right! Those are all important parts of our process.
Punihei:	Time for you to do the birthday party circuit!
Bubba:	Yes dear. I can't wait.
Punihei:	I'm so tired. I'm so proud of you and I'm a little jealous. But I'm super proud of you. Now we need to go to sleep. Good night.
Bubba:	Good night. *Aloha wau iā ʻoe* (I love you).
Punihei:	*Aloha wau iā ʻoe pū.*

CHAPTER 13

THE JUGGLING ACT

Finding Work-Life Balance with a Little Help!

Bibiana Mancera

Life has always been a balancing act. My earliest recollections as a child were watching my parents balance work-life, for them it was family and work. Both of my parents worked in the public sector to maintain the household. This was during a time when women were supposed to stay at home to care for the children. In retrospect, watching that as a child left such an impact on me, it was the norm, for my siblings and me. Hence, I learned the juggling act model from my parents; working different shifts, being left with my grandparents, being dropped off and picked up from school, working in the home, cooking and cleaning, and attending mass. All of these experiences formed the intricate patterns of my life. As a child, I always sought more of everything, knowledge, family, friends, food, and love and not necessarily in this order. These things have always brought me joy and comfort. But it is the quest for knowledge that has inspired me to become more. Never in my wildest dreams did I ever think I would be where I am today, working on a PhD at the age of 46, with two children, Marcos (10 years) and Isabella (3 years). Most people my age are at the stage in life where they already have established careers, are seeing their kids off to college, or becoming grandparents. I, on the other hand, barely realized a few years ago what I wanted to be when I

Beyond the Pride and the Privilege: The Stories of Doctoral Students and Work-Life Balance, pages 83–90.

grew up. I guess you can say I am a late bloomer and a non-traditional student, but that is okay. I'm very comfortable with both of those titles. I have always been the type of person that had to be active and participate in many different things at the same time, whether it was family, work, school, church, or community. These self-imposed activities have driven my expectations of who I am and who I want to be, but I guess that is the way it was meant to be. Because of this I am often caught struggling to find a work life balance. The demands on my time have increased exponentially as my children have grown and as I seek a PhD.

I embarked on the path to attaining a PhD in 2012, with the encouragement of my boss, Dr. Elias Provencio-Vasquez, the UTEP Dean of the School of Nursing and Principal Investigator of the Hispanic Health Disparities Research Center. He is flexible with my schedule, allows me to take courses during the day if needed, and work on school related items during the course of my day as long as I do my job as Project Manager. I am fortunate to have a boss who sees me as a professional and values my work. So, I always respond to his emails and work requests even when I am at home with a sick child. Support, in balancing work life, truly comes in all forms, from a simple gesture like a text message telling me that I am capable of getting a PhD, or even an encouraging conversation when I am having trouble figuring out a statistical assignment. I try and follow these examples and do so by encouraging others in similar situations to believe in themselves and continue with their education no matter how challenging it may seem at the moment.

In my latest educational endeavor of working towards a PhD, managing my time is critical; relying on support systems indispensable; and finding balance is essential. My education has really come one degree at a time with help from my family and friends, beginning with my husband (Ray), who started my journey in higher education when we first started dating. Ray literally made an appointment with a friend of his, who was the Assistant Dean of Students, at the University of Texas at El Paso (UTEP). The purpose of this meeting was so that I could get a lecture about the value of an education and how to start the admissions process. I knew then Ray was a keeper! Thirteen years later, in 2005, I was married to Ray and the mother of Marcos (2 yrs). I was a student affairs coordinator for a Master in Public Health (MPH) program, counseling and helping students get an MPH. I thought to myself, "What am I doing, helping all these people get a Master's degree and I don't even have one?" It didn't take me long to realize I was in a dead-end job, with no upward mobility. So, I had a discussion with my husband concerning my career advancement. The only way to do so was through education, by attaining a Master's Degree. Ray said "go for it 150%." He agreed to rearrange his schedule to take care of Marcos when I had class, homework, projects, or to study. We managed to get through a Master's degree literally working as a "tag-team," juggling our schedules between family, work, church, and school. The tag-team approach has really been our lifesaver in terms of balancing work-life. We truly created a partnership. Without my husband's support, I would not be in school today.

Fast-forward 2012, Ray and I had another discussion about my career, and this time we discussed the importance of a PhD in order to become a National Institutes of Health (NIH) Center Director. At this juncture in my life, I am the mother of two children Marcos (10) and Isabella (3) At this juncture in my life, as a mother with a career focus, the demands on my time are even greater, but I continue to rely on the tag-team approach to balance my time between family, work, and school. Thank God I still have the support of my husband who is self-employed, but works longer hours in order to keep up with his clients and attend all the meetings of the organizations he belongs to.

THE DAILY GRIND, THE ROUTINE OF A DOCTORAL STUDENT

In order to keep my sanity and maintain a work-life balance, I must make light of my situation. For those of you who have children, you will completely understand what I am about to describe, and for those who are anticipating children in the future, get ready for the fun!

I lovingly refer to my day as shift-work. Shift one typically starts between 5:45 a.m. and 6:30 a.m., depending on whether or not I had a decent night's sleep (sleep has now become a luxury). I prepare breakfast, finish packing lunches, clean-up and try to eat breakfast while I'm doing everything else (literally standing by the kitchen sink and counter). On days that my husband can help with the kids, I have about 20 extra minutes to get ready. If on the one hand I have to take both kids to school and daycare, then by 7:00 a.m. I must hit the shower and be out the door no later than 7:35 a.m., in order to get my son to school by 7:45 a.m. I then drive across town to drop off my three year old daughter at daycare, which is seven minutes away from the university, and try to make it into my office between 8:15 a.m. and 8:30 a.m.

Shift two begins once I arrive at work, which is sometimes a reprieve from shift one, depending on the moods of my children. I usually don't leave the building until the end of the day. I multi-task all day long between work tasks and school related items. Luckily, most of my work can be addressed from my desk or via email. My lunch hour is reserved for school-work (reading, homework, and assignments) and on a rare occasion when I really need a mental break, I leave the confines of the building and grab something to eat, just to get away and clear my mind. Evenings when I have class, I rely on my husband to pick up the kids and take care of them until I get home around 8:00 p.m. Most days, my husband usually picks up my son from school in the afternoon; however, there are quite a few evenings that he has meetings, so I must make other arrangements for the kids. On the evenings I don't have class; I try and stay until 5:45 p.m. to work on school-related items because I have to pick my daughter up by 6:00 p.m. from daycare and my son from my husband's office thereafter.

Shift three begins when I have the kids in tow. Once we arrive at home, if I don't have to go to the grocery store, I either begin dinner, warm up something I have prepared ahead of time, or enjoy something I have left cooking in the crock-pot. Once the kids and I eat, usually without my husband, who typically arrives around 8:00 p.m., we begin my son's homework. This in itself is a daunting task, balancing two very different personalities. One child challenges me mentally and the other physically. Marcos is my mental challenge. He is a gifted and talented child, who is very intelligent but despises homework and more so because it usually entails writing, which he sees no point in doing. He would be perfectly content if every subject were math and science. To complicate things a little more, Marcos is in a dual language program where he receives 80% of his schooling in Spanish, 15% in English, and 5% in Japanese (his elective). All of this must be done while keeping my daughter Isabella out of Marcos' hair and out of any mischief. Isabella is my physical challenge, you would think after chasing her around for a couple of hours every day, I would be physically fit, not the case at all! I must admit that taking classes for the PhD has really prepared me to deal with the questions my son asks and the concepts he is taught at school. My study time at home is limited to the hour or so before we all go to sleep; this is the time I read, after I have finished in the kitchen preparing lunches for the next day and cleaning up.

As I have gotten older, I can no longer pull all-nighters studying, so I have to make all my time count. This is especially so on weekends. If I have not advanced a great deal on studies during the week, I do so on the weekends. Since my husband is self-employed, he usually works on weekends as well, so we have to plan ahead. Saturdays are reserved for my son's chess tournaments, which can last between five and six hours. This is an opportunity for me to catch up on homework. Unless of course I have Isabella with me, if not, I spend all my time chasing her around and taking her to the newly discovered restrooms. The rest of my Saturday is spent running errands, grocery shopping, doing laundry, cooking, and or cleaning. Sundays are a bit more relaxed. If I wake before the rest of my family, I read or work on homework for a couple of hours until I hear the kids come down for breakfast. Sundays are when we all spend time together. We have a large breakfast, and get ready for church. I usually try and prepare lunch before we leave for mass at 12:15 p.m. After mass, if I don't have lunch ready, we go out to eat, go home, relax, and watch movies. But when someone gets sick, or my husband leaves town for business, this all goes out the window and I go to plan b, drop everything to focus on the kids. I may not cook most of our meals, and if I do cook, they are fairly simple and I forget about cleaning, unless I'm really inspired to do it. This is how I try to balance school and family.

Oftentimes, my schedule and my husband's don't lend themselves to tag-teaming. This is when I have come to rely on my other support systems (parents and siblings) and ask for help. I was never one to ask for any assistance because I suffer from the "oldest child" syndrome. From an early age, this enabled me to take charge of things, my siblings, chores, and school-work. It is quite different now that I am working on a PhD. I no longer have the energy or sufficient time to do all things and be all things to everyone in my life, but that's alright. I no longer campaign for political elections or attend League of United Latin American Citizen

(LULAC) meetings. I rarely go to dinner with my husband alone and I no longer take weekend get-a-ways with my husband. I have relinquished many activities in order to keep my sanity, find balance, and enjoy life. I'm not going to say that I'm not stressed out at times, but at least I know I can count on my parents and siblings, and I am not doing this alone. This is essential for me.

FAMILY IS A GREAT SUPPORT SYSTEM

My parents, Raymond and Diana, now in their 70s, have been quite a blessing in my life as well. They have always been there to support my siblings and me as well as to help care for our children. They have taught me to do things with love and understanding. My mother's mantra "do all things with love, even the cooking, cleaning, and laundry," is taken from Mother Theresa's saying, "In this life we cannot do great things. We can only do small things with great love," has gotten me through moments when I am overwhelmed trying to find my work life balance. Hearing my mother's voice, in my mind, reminds of the undying commitment, tenacity, and love required to raise a family, work, and attend school. I am also blessed to have a sister, Claudia who helps me when my husband can't or is out of town. She will take care of one or both of my kids when I have class, homework, projects, or church related obligations. I used to help my sister with her daughters when I was single and had no children. Perhaps, this is her way of paying me back. I like to think it is because she finds her niece and nephew adorable! My brother, Raymond, and my sister-in-law, Jennifer, are also God-sent, they help me out by keeping my son overnight or inviting him over to spend time with their three boys. In my culture we say "echando la mano" (giving a helping hand). This is something I grew up seeing within my extended family; the willingness of my aunts and uncles to support each other by caring for each other's children. When someone was in a bind, they always stepped in to lend a hand. Knowing that I can always count on my family for a helping hand and support helps me balance all aspects of my busy life.

FAITH IS A ROCK AND FOUNDATION FOR BALANCE

Another huge component of my work-life balance is my faith. I have always found solace in it, yet I know that many people don't believe in the concept of God, especially in graduate school because we are taught to think critically and question. Personally, faith has brought me great comfort and peace in times of sadness and stress. It is one of the major ways I deal with stress and how I manage to maintain my inner balance; without it I could not balance any other aspect of my life. I have been a music minister since I was 15 years old, which leads me to one of my other support systems, my choir, who are like a second family to me. I have sung with them for the past 25 years. The time I spend with my choir is when I decompress because I am doing something I love, singing. Rehearsals are a time for me to get away from my family, work, and school. It is my time, when I feed my soul. My choir is always there for each other and we have sung at each others' weddings, family funerals, baptisms, and other special events. We sing, laugh, talk, pray, and sing some more. Prayer and music have the ability to calm me and to center me when I am out of focus. Prayer is truly the rock on which my life is balanced upon. Prayer for me is a powerful tool that I use on a daily basis. Music is the other form of prayer I rely on, as St. Augustine of Hippo so succinctly stated "He who sings well, prays twice." The lyrics of the songs we sing on Sundays and special occasions minister not only to our assembly, but oftentimes to me as well. When I need a mental break, I play liturgical music and listen to the words with my heart and frequently cry. I cry out of joy, knowing how truly blessed I am, or because it is a catharsis to purge all of my frustration and stress. Then I am able to focus on the task or issue at hand, thus my faith is at the core of finding balance in my life.

DIFFICULT CHOICES PHD STUDENTS MAKE

I have come to realize many things, as I have gotten older; finding balance in my life is about so many things. Things that mattered when I was younger no longer do, and things I never gave much importance to are now much more relevant. Take for example, when I was in my early twenties, I didn't think twice about staying out late and sleeping only a few hours, now without sleep I don't function. I would not have thought twice about eating just about every meal out, now food is what must nourish my body and keep me healthy, so my choices are much more sound and nutritious. I no longer worry about my weight and appearance, as I once did, because after two children delivered by C-section, I will never fit into my size six jeans and that's alright. As long as I am not diagnosed with diabetes, cardio-vascular disease, or high blood pressure, and I have the energy to keep up with my children, then all is well. Nothing in life will ever be perfect and nature never intended it that way. Just knowing that is comfort in itself. I try to avoid being the "superwoman," defined by Merriam Webster as an exceptional woman, especially: a woman who succeeds in having a career and raising a family because of all the expectations and unnecessary pressure. I don't believe it is truly possible. The closest we can come to being a superwoman is by finding a work-life balance. Perhaps it is by discarding activities that aren't important, and by continuing to do things that are important; in other words, prioritizing.

FAMILY LIFE

One of my major priorities has always been family and the responsibilities of a household. My family is what my work-life balance revolves around. Having been raised in a traditional Mexican-American family, from an early age I learned how to cook, clean, and care for my family from the best (my grandmothers, mother, and aunts). My childhood recollections of all these women are imbedded in who I am today. I must admit that the cooking is what I enjoy the most because I love food and food nourishes my family. My maternal grandfather was raised in Durango, Mexico and was not wealthy by any means, so for him to see a thin child meant there was not enough food in the house. He always ensured that his family of ten children and my grandmother had more than enough to eat. My ideas of caring for people come from him. Food is an important part of my culture and a way of taking care of my family. I know many women don't enjoy cooking, but I do. In order to balance work life, I try to prepare meals over the weekend or on nights that I don't have class. I usually fix 3–4 meals in advance. The crock-pot has become my best friend and making extra food and freezing has been a life-saver. Part of my helping hand philosophy includes preparing enough food for my parents and siblings to give them a break, especially when I have days off. This is one way I take care of one of my huge support systems.

SUPPORT AT WORK AND SCHOOL

My support system at work and school is comprised of my boss, co-workers, colleagues, and professors. They are my mentors and more importantly friends who understand the value of an education. Since the majority of them are PhDs, they have been in my situation trying to achieve a work life balance. I know how fortunate I am to be surrounded by them because they challenge me mentally, guide me, listen to me, and support my efforts to balance family, work, and school. Without all their help and understanding I would not be working on a PhD. It is a very strenuous endeavor. The amount of time I devote to reading, writing, assignments, and projects is unbelievable; unless you are in a PhD program can you fully comprehend what I am referring to. In my first semester, I had a melt-down. I was having problems with statistical equations, I was missing my children's school events, and feeling overwhelmed. I hadn't had a statistics course in over 15 years. Statistics were literally Greek to me. So, I went to speak to my biostatics professor because I did not understand the coursework. I really thought about dropping the course and even the program, which really made me feel even worse. I felt like a failure. Luckily, my professor understood what was going on and she began to explain the issues she had faced in her PhD program. I realized I was not alone in feeling the way I was. She then discussed the rigors of a PhD and what implications it would have on my work life balance. She said one of her mentors told her that attaining a PhD was the second hardest thing next to boot camp and serving in the military. I had no idea until mid-semester what she was referring to. I found myself preparing for mid-terms, working on projects, and homework, asking myself what I was doing in a PhD program at my age with all my work and family commitments. Then I remembered the second part of our conversation; to always keep in the back of my mind what my motivation was in seeking a PhD. That was easy, my children, husband, and parents. I count my blessings every day for my support systems. I know many students are not as fortunate.

There is such peace in knowing that I am not alone and I can ask for help. For the longest time, I felt guilty asking for help and thought I had to do everything by myself. Then I remembered John Donne, the famous English poet who wrote

Devotions upon Emergent Occasions in 1624: "No man is an island, Entire of itself, Each is a piece of the continent, A part of the main" {sic}. This quote is a constant reminder that I can't do this alone and that I can count on my husband, parents, siblings, friends, and colleagues; all I need to do is ask.

Perhaps it is my age, wisdom, or seeing my mother and listening to her advice of not to follow her footsteps in trying to be a superwoman as we discuss her health. As a result, that forces me to take a good, hard look at myself. She tells me "learn from my mistakes, unless you want to end up like me, with my health issues." This is a valuable lesson I am still trying to learn. It is difficult to balance work life because for someone like me, who is the oldest, independent, and driven; the thought of failure is almost inconceivable. This is a particularly challenging concept for me because I have always strived to do my best in everything. My saving grace is that I am not a perfectionist; if I were, maintaining a work life balance would be impossible. I know I will never be the best wife, mother, student, housekeeper, cook, or music liturgist, but I will have the privilege of attempting all of them and being successful at all or most.

Life in general is about balance of mind, body and soul; work life; yin and yang; positive and negative etc… I think I am on my way to mastering two, mind and soul, and the third component, the body, is one I must work harder at integrating. In terms of work life, I have learned to ask for help, especially when I feel overwhelmed. The more you dream of accomplishing, the more difficult it becomes.

If things had happened differently in my life, for example graduating from college right after high school, or having my kids at a much earlier age, I don't believe I would have been mature enough, wise enough, or tough enough to endure all of the intricacies of maintaining a work life balance. It is a culmination of life's experiences, my upbringing, and years of trial and error that have brought me to where I am today. I have fully embraced who I am, a woman, Hispanic, daughter, sister, wife, mother, friend, professional, and life-long student. Understanding this is part of mentally balancing work life because each title carries different responsibilities and various amounts of time to fulfill. But the greatest satisfaction for me is knowing that I am beating the odds, one degree at a time, with a little help from my family and friends.

CHAPTER 14

MI VIDA LOCA

My Crazy Life As A Full-Time Doctoral Student

Edna Martinez

"You need a life!" he said as I headed back into Tillman Hall, the very building students, staff, and a few faculty members were scurrying out of to begin the weekend. "This *is* my life. I put my life on hold for this," I hastily retorted. To his defense, his statement was not one of criticism, but rather concern. The same concern expressed by other friends and family, and more loudly echoed by my mother during our daily phone conversations. I may not make my bed, take out the trash, check the mail, or exercise on a daily basis, but the one thing I am consistent about is speaking on the phone with my mother, my rock. These conversations can be a short and sweet 10 minutes or go well past 30 minutes, make that 60 minutes if my niece and nephews are around. Frankly, I'd be lying if I said she has my undivided attention the entire time—of this, I am certain she is fully aware. In addition to catching up on the latest going on at home, during this time I also manage to watch the local news, reply to a few emails, cook, and eat dinner before heading back to campus. Well, maybe not cook, but more so prepare myself a sandwich or pour a bowl of cereal. And yes, I will admit, ramen noodles. I find it necessary to indicate *instant* ramen noodles because while I've been locked up in Tillman Hall, ramen has come to reign beyond the walls of college residence halls and onto

Beyond the Pride and the Privilege: The Stories of Doctoral Students and Work-Life Balance, pages 91–95.

high-end menus. In any case, our mother-daughter phone calls usually end with "*Te Amo*[1]," but not before a bit of scolding for my lack of rest, eating right, and of course, late nights in Tillman Hall. *Estás loca*[2], she often says. "I know," I reply.

Tillman Hall is home to Clemson University's School of Education and thus the place where I spend most of my time. If any of my peers get locked out of the building, I'm usually the first person they text asking "You in Tillman?" At times it is clear they are seeking confirmation rather than inquiring. Tillman is also the person I joke about having a date with. If I ever get bored or tired of Tillman, I can always depend on Cooper, also known as the library.

Evidently, based on this long introduction I may not be the most appropriate person to write about work-life balance. Candidly, if I were writing this chapter my first year, I would adamantly proclaim that work-life balance does not exist. Nonetheless, at this point in my doctoral studies I believe I've achieved a comfortable "balance." Perfect? No, but certainly mentally, physically, spiritually, and emotionally healthier. While continuing to fulfill doctorate level expectations, I now sleep a little more, exercise more frequently, and do more of the things I enjoy. I missed live music, biking, and hiking—all things I put on hold. More recently, I've taken up kickboxing. There is something extremely addicting and therapeutic about punching the hell out of a bag; although truthfully in my head it's not always a bag! Yes, I still leave my apartment in the morning with tousled wet hair and little to no makeup, but hey I made it to the meeting on time, didn't I? I'll take an extra 30 minutes of sleep over blow-drying my hair and failed efforts to reduce the dark circles under my eyes any day.

With a never-ending to-do list, upcoming internship, and expected dissertation research-related travel, I've questioned why I agreed to write a chapter, let alone seek to serve as an editor for the book. As Sweet Brown would say "Ain't nobody got time for that!" Then again, as someone interested in pursuing the professoriate I understand the need to publish. Lately, Sweet Brown has become the most often cited person by other research assistants in my program of study—yes, more than Kezar *and* Gasman combined. If you've been buried under articles and data trying to finish up conference proposals for the University Council for Educational Administration and Association for the Study of Higher Education conventions, not yet having fully recovered from the American Educational Research Association annual meeting, you're probably wondering "who is Sweet Brown?" YouTube it! There's a 42 second minute clip—short enough not to cause feelings of guilt for wasting time. Yes, I often speak of time as a commodity and live by Weber's (1930/2002) notion that "*wasting time* is...the first and most serious of all sins" (p. 106). I've lived according to this particular belief most of my time as a doctoral student; however, my understanding of "wasting time" has evolved each year.

My first year was the most challenging in terms of work-life balance. My view of "wasting time" involved everything outside of school. I occasionally hung out with my peers, slept in, even went on a few hiking trips, but was quickly consumed with guilt. I reminded myself that I had resigned from my professional position at The University of Texas at El Paso (UTEP) and relocated to South Carolina for the PhD, not to explore the Appalachian Trail. My initial obsession with time and working incessantly was in part related to my connection with our program coordinator at the time, who had been my professor and mentor during my graduate studies at UTEP. In the back of my mind I wondered if my peers and faculty especially, saw me as capable and deserving of being in the program or simply as his recruit.

To this point, my first year was focused on proving that I deserved to be at Clemson. The fact that I was the *first* Latina admitted into our program also made me work feverishly. For me, being a "first" came with additional, primarily self-imposed, responsibilities. It wasn't just about proving myself, but also debunking myths about Latino higher education abilities and aspirations. I also viewed my acceptance into the program as an opportunity to highlight that the quality of education/preparation I received at a less renowned Hispanic Serving Institution, paralleled, and in several instances surpassed that of the more prestigious colleges and universities attended by some of my peers.

Initially, for example, I oftentimes found myself "educating" people about the heterogeneity of the Latino population, problems of essentializing, and responding to stereotypes. Candidly, in some cases I realized some individuals were not worth my limited time and energy. Exhausted and stunned by the ignorance, I defeatedly accepted that some folks would never "get it" or simply did not care to "get it." To date, I clearly recall having to clarify to a peer that being Mexican American did not mean one of my parents was White and the other Mexican. As our conversation continued, from my perspective, it became evident that it was difficult for them to conceive that someone with two Latino parents had reached my level of educational attainment and that my parents were indeed my greatest source of support.

Despite common assumptions that Latino families often serve as a barrier to students' educational aspirations, throughout my studies, my family has been most protective of my time, wellbeing, and peace of mind. For example, my parents have forbidden my siblings to notify me of any issues that arise back at home, particularly in terms of their health. Relatedly, my strength and ability to balance life and work was tested my second year as a doctoral student. Two weeks into the 2012 spring semester, after recently ringing in the New Year with my family in El Paso, I received one of those dreaded phone calls you hope to never receive. My father was in critical condition in the hospital with little chance of survival. After an emotional breakdown in Tillman Hall, frantically searching for the earliest flight home, informing my faculty that I was not sure if and when I would be back, packing a change of clothes in my backpack, the longest ride to the airport, and five hour flight home, I made it to the hospital where my family and I spent a month pacing back and forth in an intensive care unit waiting room.

Respectfully refusing to let me withdraw from school, my advisor and mentors moved swiftly to help me make arrangements with faculty whose courses

I was currently enrolled in. While taking shifts in the hospital with other family members, I strived to remain on track. I was thankful when, for example, one faculty member allowed me to conduct field observations for my qualitative research course at the hospital, rather than an educational setting. I was late on several Blackboard discussion posts for my other classes and they certainly weren't representative of my best work, but they got done.

Some days I had full faith in God that my dad would pull through. Other days I lost all hope, especially when family I had never met, the hospital chaplain, and multiple employees started to visit, and in some cases say their goodbyes. Given that the hospital was also my father's place of employment, we were never alone, which sometimes is exactly what I wanted. I wanted to be alone to cry, pray, meditate, and oh yes, read. After all, I was still enrolled in school. After a month of back and forth between the ICU and operating room, my dad was on his way to a slow recovery. And I was on my way back to a slow start at Clemson. Although I was not ready to come back, my mother and siblings forced me back.

This experience led me to the realization that my life did not have to be put on hold simply because I was working towards obtaining a PhD. I was able to manage life, family, school, work, emotions, among other things during one of the most trying moments in my life; thus, surely I did not have to live in Tillman. I began to establish boundaries and take agency. I also began doing things that were important to me outside of my role as a doctoral student. I found and created spaces where I could serve in meaningful ways, such as mentoring first-generation undergraduate Latinas and establishing relationships with their parents. Stronger and more personal relationships with my advisor and supervising faculty also contributed to my ability to achieve a healthier work-life balance.

During my first year when I was given a work assignment I would tire myself to get it done immediately even if it meant staying up till four in the morning. Once again, this was associated with the idea that I needed to prove myself. Clearly it wasn't something they expected. Although images of demanding, uncaring, and rigid faculty are all too familiar, such was not my case. The more comfortable I got, I was able to ask for clear deadlines and express concerns about my ability to get it done by the desired deadline. Previously, I would never admit such thing as I viewed it as a sign a weakness. Today, I view it as a sign of my growth and development, both personally and professionally. Evidently, working with others makes work-life balance work!

My dad's hospitalization further reinforced the importance of family and a new understanding of what "wasting time" entailed. More than ever I realized that I did not have to put my personal life on hold. In other words unlike previously, I became open to the idea of dating, going out, and meeting new people. Before leaving El Paso, I made a conscious effort to avoid starting a serious relationship. First, a long distance relationship was out of the question and besides school was to be my priority. Sincerely, given my new perspective, I've had the opportunity to meet great people, but have found it difficult to foster a relationship with my better, yet still unbalanced life. Turns out when you're dating someone, they actually want to see you and unless they are also enrolled in a doctorate program will rarely understand your crazy life. Additionally, it wouldn't hurt to blow-dry your hair and put on some makeup every now and then. You may also call it selfishness, but after a long day sometimes the thing you desire most is solitude. Nothing better than going home, pouring a glass of wine, and listening to Norah Jones's "The Long Day is Over," until of course you realize the day is far from over!

CHAPTER 15

RAISING DIEGO

Work Is Work, Family Is Everything

Marlen Kanagui-Muñoz and José Muñoz

While we knew we really wanted children for the majority of our six-year relationship, we also had dreams of earning our PhDs in fields we loved. Although we always placed family first, we knew it was important for us to achieve our personal goals so that we could be truly happy in parenthood. We wanted to travel, spend time together, have fun with our friends, and just enjoy being 20-somethings before our family grew. As two doctoral students, we knew that transitioning into parenthood would not be easy given the rigor and expectations associated with becoming a scholar. Yet, driven by our decision to not lose sight of our dreams for a family, we utilized our doctoral student know-how, mixed with a little creativity and resourcefulness, to embark on the most challenging and rewarding chapter of our lives to date.

TO PARENT OR NOT TO PARENT: DECIDING TO HAVE A FAMILY

Our decision to enter parenthood while in graduate school was largely influenced by discussions we had with others that had children before and after graduate school. The consensus was that there is "never a perfect time" to have children.

Beyond the Pride and the Privilege: The Stories of Doctoral Students and Work-Life Balance, pages 97–103.

Surprisingly, many fellow graduate students and professors shared that graduate school was actually a great time for parenthood given that graduate school can often be more flexible than full-time employment or the early tenure process. We took all this information in, weighed our options, and thought about what would make us happy. We took a little leap of faith and decided it was time; we would try for a baby in graduate school.

Our initial joy was quickly accompanied by the thought that we had to begin planning for baby, which if not regulated, can easily become overwhelming. In the process of researching and preparing for parenthood as graduate students, we came to the realization that it is impossible to plan for it all. We knew that while we could try our best to prepare, there was a part of parenthood that we had to jump into and trust that we had what it takes to be parents. Just like working on a research project, we knew that in addition to extensive research, there is a certain amount of intuitiveness in the problem-solving process. With that in mind, we chose to focus on two main areas we felt were most important: finances and self-care.

It is no secret that graduate student salaries are not the most lucrative; often requiring a certain amount of financial creativity to make ends meet. We were fortunate to have graduate student health insurance, covered by our research assistantships, which covered a large amount of the pregnancy-related costs. We worked out a payment plan for the remainder of the costs. We have to admit, it was a little strange to give payments for the birth of our son, but after six monthly payments our son was all ours! We also took advantage of state and federal support programs, such as state-funded health insurance for Diego, the Parents as Teachers Program, and Women, Infants, and Children (WIC).

Another important aspect of preparing our lives to welcome a baby was to focus on our own health and self-care. We got our yearly health checks, started eating better, and made better efforts to incorporate exercise into our lives. Another important thing to regulate during pre-pregnancy and pregnancy stress, which is easier said than done in graduate school! Although we couldn't eliminate stress, we could increase activities to combat it. We made efforts to find time to do things together and alone that had absolutely nothing to do with research or graduate school. We also had to make professional sacrifices like extending our graduation timelines knowing that our transition into parenthood would require time and attention. Being intentional about taking care of ourselves was an important step in preparing our mind, body, and spirit to welcome a new life into our home.

BALANCING BABY

It's amazing how one little line can change your entire life in an instant. On July 29, 2011, we learned from a home pregnancy test that we were pregnant. Although, we were trying to get pregnant, we still stood at the bathroom sink wide-eyed and stunned. We had just received the biggest responsibility of our lives—creating and protecting a life. We were fortunate to have a relatively uncomplicated pregnancy and birth. On April 12th, after a 12-hour natural labor, our son Diego came into the world.

Although our hearts were so ready to welcome Diego, the first few weeks were tough. We read the books and took all the baby classes, but our lives had changed drastically overnight and we just had to cope the best way we could. Although Diego is what people call an "easy baby" (i.e., no colic, breast-fed like champ, and slept long stretches), some nights we wondered what we were thinking. What made us think that we could be parents? You need a license to drive, but do they just let anyone have a child? The fact that our parents could only stay for two weeks postpartum made things even more difficult. Once they left to California again, we felt truly alone and overwhelmed with responsibility. While Marlen had finished her semester early due to the delivery, José still had to finish classes and exams. In addition to all the work, we had to battle sleep deprivation, playing the why-is-the-baby-crying guessing game several times a day, and, for Marlen, the hormonal changes of postpartum and the joys of early breastfeeding.

Childcare

We made the decision to forgo outside childcare and tag-team care between the two of us. One of the major factors in this decision was that it did not make financial sense to pay for daycare since the cost per month roughly equaled one of our graduate assistantship stipends. Although we have enjoyed caring for our son, this decision was tedious. In short, anytime one of us is working whether on- or off-campus, the other is with the baby. As you could imagine for two graduate students in the middle of comprehensive exams, with full course loads, teaching and research responsibilities, and dissertations in progress, it was quite a feat! We often wonder what our neighbors think as they see our cars come in and out of our driveway several times a day! Graduate students often worry about having enough time to parent, which we think is a legitimate concern. However, we believe that graduate school can be a fantastic time to parent as well. Although we work roughly 40–50 hours, these hours are flexible. Yes, that means working late at night and early mornings, but nobody said it would be easy.

Communication

Balancing the responsibility of a baby has increased our need to communicate and work together effectively. Take for example our first family trip to the supermarket. We got the baby ready, packed the diaper bag, loaded the stroller, and got into the car. About an hour later, we finally arrived at the store and began browsing the baby section. Diego decided to have a giant "blowout" and there was poop everywhere— on his stroller, up his back, and all over us! We had what Tim Gunn would call a "make it work" moment. We agreed that Jose would check our items out, while Marlen took the baby back to the car to begin the diaper change. We learned a lot from our first family outing. We had to work together, take care of business, and in the end, we had to laugh at our baby and ourselves as we frantically changed our baby in the backseat of our car. Since then, we have had to come together numerous times to negotiate time to complete our graduate work and the responsibilities related to caring for our son. We have used multiple strategies to make sure that we continue to stay connected as a couple, engaged as parents, and focused as graduate students.

Forging New Paths, Connecting to our Past

As first-generation graduate students, we've had to figure out many things on our own. Parenting in graduate school was by far uncharted territory. We have had to forge new definitions of what it means to be a "mom" or "dad" as our situation is vastly different from that of our parents. As such, it's been critical to find mentors and fellow graduate school parents to supplement the support of our families. For example, during her first semester back at school, Marlen met regularly with a professor who had also recently become a mother. They would take out the strollers and talk about career issues, research, babies, and everything in between. Seeking support from others, even those who weren't parents was an important part of finding our balance. Parenting has renewed our relationships with our family in new and exciting ways. We see our parents in a new light and they see us in a different way as well. It has been so important for us to stay connected with our families and complement our "evidence-based" parenting approach with the wisdom of our mothers and fathers.

Perfect Parenting is an Oxymoron

As graduate students, many of us often struggle with perfectionistic tendencies. While perfectionism can be adaptive at times, it can also be maladaptive, paralyzing, and stress inducing. When you stare into your baby's eyes for the first time, you wonder how you'll make your surroundings equally perfect. The bottom line is that we can't control everything and perhaps we shouldn't. During the past year, it has been so important to remind ourselves to be gentle with ourselves, especially when we make mistakes. We still remember the first time Diego bumped his head because we were trying to take a picture of him. It seems silly now, but we got so scared that we called the hospital nurse line to make sure he was okay. Since then there have been numerous stress and guilt inducing moments. We still struggle with the urge to be "perfect parents," but are coming to the understanding that we have to do the best we can with what we have. We will make mistakes— just like our parents and their parents—but we will recover and perhaps in watching this dance, our son will learn to succeed and fail with some amount of grace, too.

NOTES TO GRADUATE STUDENTS AND DEPARTMENTS

In this section we would like to humbly offer some suggestions to fellow graduate students, their families, and university departments. The following suggestions are made with the understanding that one-size does not fit all and that graduate students are in the best position to make decisions about their readiness to start a family.

For Graduate Students

- *Be intentional about caring for your relationships.* The old proverb of "it takes a village to raise a child" has rung true for us. Although we are away from our families, we have developed a core group of friends, mentors, and academic *familia* (family) who have been our support system during this transition. Also, intentionally setting time for each other has been paramount to parenting effectively. While the tasks of caring for a baby can make a relationship take a turn for the mundane, it's important to find time to nurture your relationship. Since both time and money were limited, we would have movie nights at home or make copycat recipes from our favorite restaurants while the baby was sleeping.
- *Assess and then reassess.* As graduate students, we are familiar with evaluations and assessment in a variety of forms. Taking some of these "How's my driving?" skills into our personal lives can be very important. In graduate school, it is easy to go on autopilot and continue to do things that perhaps are not working. At the end of each semester, we go out for dinner or prepare something special at home and talk about the best and the worst part of the semester. We also talk about our hopes and wishes for the next one. What did we do well? What didn't work? What can we do better?
- *Connect with other parents.* Make an effort to find outlets on campus or in the community to talk to other parents. Although we have the skills to Google everything to death and research intensely, sometimes it's as easy as asking a fellow parent, "Did that diaper rash cream work for you?" Commiserating with other parents or even exchanging a knowing look can do wonders for your spirit.
- *Taking care of yourself!* Parenting takes a huge emotional and physical toll on our bodies. Women experience profound changes physically during pregnancy, childbirth, and nursing. The demands of a new baby may have you losing sleep and experiencing higher than usual stress levels. Think about the things that made you happy before baby (e.g., talking with friends, going to the gym, reading for leisure) and try to find ways to gently incorporate them in your life again. Sometimes it was helpful for us to tell each other out loud what we needed that week, (e.g., "I really need a haircut soon; do. Do you think we can carve some time out for that this week?")

For Graduate Departments

- *Acknowledge the bump.* Pregnancy and childbirth is a very personal decision and process. For this reason, both graduate students and advisors alike may struggle to find ways to broach the topic. We've heard stories of graduate students "hiding" their pregnancies for as long as possible because they feared rejection or judgment from their colleagues and advisors. Ignoring a student's pregnancy or failing to entertain concerns about family planning may send the message that this part of your student's life is not relevant to their overall academic and career satisfaction. It's also important to check assumptions about family planning. For example, assuming that your female graduate student has family planning concerns or assuming that your male graduate student does not, may both be equally harmful to the student.
- *Assess departmental family friendliness.* Does your department invite spouses and children to departmental gatherings? Are people encouraged to share good news regarding family events on departmental listservs? Are women given appropriate accommodations to nurse or change their children? These are just a few of the questions that may make a world of difference to graduate students starting their families. It's important to acknowledge that students may not directly ask about the family friendliness of departments, but rather look to small indicators to assess the culture of the department. Finally, any good assessment starts with taking a good look at ourselves. We've all received societal messages about work and family. It may be important to question if you hold any assumptions or biases (i.e., a mother's place is in the home, paternity leave is not necessary) that you may be inadvertently acting from. Where did these messages come from and how can you help to dismantle them within yourself and your department?
- *Encourage work-life balance for everyone in the department.* What are the expectations for graduate students in your department? Are they manageable for graduate students with families? For example, are meetings scheduled during times that may coincide with regular familial time commitments (e.g., when school lets out)? We all know that the life of an academic is anything but easy, but that does not mean it has to be all consuming. Graduate students, much like many faculty, regularly struggle with deciding how to manage their time in order to feel productive, while still taking care of their personal needs. Include the responsibility of parenting and the flexibility of any free time is limited further, often resulting in the sacrificing of personal time. Acknowledging other time commitments and encouraging students to tend to them limits much of the pressure and guilt that can come from choosing one's self and family over graduate work. Something as simple as having the flexibility to work from home can make

a huge difference, as sometimes the best time to get something done is during baby's nap time.

WHAT'S NEXT?

As we write this chapter, Marlen is completing postdoctoral interviews and Jose is writing his dissertation proposal. Diego is now 20 months, healthy, strong, and becoming very talkative. He is the highlight of our day, everyday. The past two years have been an adventure like we could have never imagined—no matter how much we prepared. As we reflect on our experience, we want to acknowledge that we write this not as a success story (we've only been parents for a short time), but as an example of one couple who chose to pursue their personal and professional goals simultaneously. There have been joys and consequences to the decision to parent during graduate school, but at the end of the day we feel we made the right decision for us. As we continue on this path, we hope to continue to strengthen our relationship, continue working towards our academic goals, and making our family and friends a priority in our lives. Although we aspire for balance, we know it is a work in progress. We liken work-life balance to the feat of a tightrope walker keeping her balance as she walks across the rope; carefully making small adjustments with each step, focusing intensely on the moment, but keeping her end goal in mind.

CHAPTER 16

ONCE UPON A TIME (THERE WAS A BALANCED LIFE)

Agustina Veny Purnamasari

So be sure when you step, step with care and great tact.
And remember that life's a great balancing act.
—*Dr. Seuss, Oh, The Places You'll Go!*

In 2010, my journey as a doctoral student began. It felt like yesterday that I arrived in the United States, trying to figure out how things are done, because everything was almost entirely different from where I came from. But it was all exciting to me.

After years of working, I finally achieved what has been my biggest dream since I was still an undergraduate student. To study in the United States. It was my father's dream too, since he never finished his college education. In our family, my sister and I were the first generation to get a college degree, and I was the first to get a Master degree. I was 16 when my mom died, and since then my dad became a single parent to my sister and me. I had seen how my dad worked, how he valued integrity and perseverance. Those were the best examples that taught me to work hard and work right. My father is always supportive of his children to pursue education. However, as much as my father wanted his children to get the best education, he could not afford to send us overseas. But, he never gave up on

Beyond the Pride and the Privilege: The Stories of Doctoral Students and Work-Life Balance, pages 105–109.

his hope and has always been supportive of mine as well. Then, in 2010 with a Fulbright scholarship, I came to the United States.

Moved to the United States

Nothing compares to the excitement of literally going to the other side of the world, to pursue the highest academic degree. Arriving in the United States was quite an adventure in itself. It was Monday, July 5, 2010, a day after the Independence Day. I was prepared with the address of the apartment that I stayed at for five weeks, the phone number of the university officer (who took care of me and other sponsored students during the five-weeks stay), but I was not prepared to find that that Monday was a holiday and that all public places, including the university and the apartment management office, were closed. So, there I was, stranded in the middle of the desert of Tucson, Arizona. Luckily, the airport shuttle bus driver helped me to find a safe hotel to stay for one night, and did not just leave me at the parking lot in front of the apartment. The five-week academic program at University of Arizona was the 'honeymoon' part of my cross-cultural adjustment; classes were fun, the sunset was beautiful, and everything was great and everyday was a sunny day in Tucson.

Pursuing the Highest Degree and Setting Your Expectations

Education is a privilege. Pursuing a doctorate degree is, therefore, a privilege of the privileged college-educated individuals. Like a pyramid, the higher the education level, the less accessible it is. A recent survey on Educational Attainment by the U.S. Census Bureau reported that only 1.6% out of 236,929,000 individuals who were ≥18 years old hold a doctorate degree (U.S. Census Bureau, 2013).

Having such a privilege to pursue a doctorate degree, hence, entails a sense of responsibility not only to my scholarship sponsor who has opened the door to this academic opportunity, but also to myself. To do more and to give the best is how I express my gratitude. However, I often set too many "targets" (i.e., papers, manuscripts, proposal, etc.) in an effort to achieve more. Like an archer who wants to shoot off the arrow, he or she focuses on a target. In the same way I should have focused on one target at a time, but I did not realize that, or maybe I overestimated my ability to multitask. So, instead of getting all works done, I missed many of the deadlines.

During the first year I spent almost all my weekends at the office. Once there was a colleague of mine who needed to take something at the office that Sunday afternoon. As soon as she opened the office, she said, "Agustina, you need to have a social life!" She was right, and it was nice of her to express her concerns of my social life, but I thought social life can wait, works on the other hand, can't.

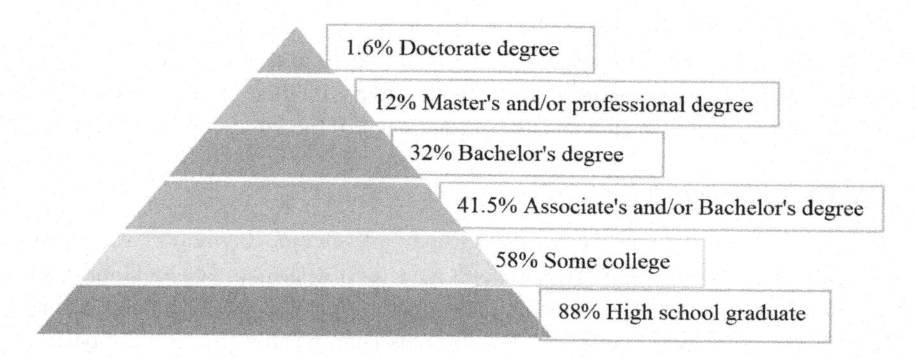

FIGURE 16.1. Pyramid of Educational Attainment (based on U.S. Census Bureau 2013 data).

The Paradox of Balance

A friend of mine mentioned about volunteering as a catechist to teach first grade students at one of the parishes in town. Before I knew how much it would help me to stay grounded, I signed up to volunteer as a catechist; and it was simply motivated by a chance to be around children. Along the way, I learned that teaching first grade students is a pleasure as well as an 'exercise' to be patient. Ever since I taught the first graders, Monday becomes the most anticipated day of the week. Somehow, the first graders become 'the energizer bunnies' who never failed to lift up my mood.

There were times when things that have past and fear of the future hold me from the present. But when I teach the first grade students, I was able to relax and be present. I guess it was because of the way the first graders enjoyed doing simple things, maybe because they were easily fascinated by things that the adults often took for granted, or because of the funny remarks they made, or the combination of all those things that gives me a bit of joy whenever I see them. Once I said to a friend, "I think the first graders are helping me, more than I'm helping them". They are truly God's sent solace. They were the first who taught me the ways to find balance.

Tips #1: Never Equate People to a Dollar Value

The saying above is among quotes I put on the wall near my desk. It reminds me to value and to nurture friendships. Friendship is priceless, too priceless to be transformed into dollar value, which can take different forms, such as, high social-status; or reputation. Time spent with or support given to our confidants, should never be converted into a dollar value. Because chances are, when you do not get the assumed-invested money, there will be nothing left, both for you and for them that can maintain the friendship. I do not know how it feels if somebody tries to assess how much advantage he hopes to get by spending time with me; neither have I wanted to know how it feels. As such, unless you are a therapist, who reasonably charges patients by the hours spent with them; please do not to try to count how money or advantage you can get out of the interactions with them.

Tips #2: At the End, It Is Not Between Me and Them

In an episode of 'Everybody Loves Raymond' sitcom, Raymond's wife said, "If you don't want to volunteer, you don't have to. It's between you and him" (her fingers pointing to the sky). To which Raymond replied, "Don't bring him into it, ok. It's not gonna work with me". But seconds later, he shouted, "Take it back!" Apparently, his wife has successfully made Raymond felt guilty for giving money instead of volunteering at the hospital. That particular line reminded me of the times when I felt some things were not right and yet, there was nothing I could do to *fix* it without taking a risk. When people did something wrong and seemed to get away with it, be patient. Like the song I liked to sing with the first graders at faith formation class, "*Be careful, for the Father up above is looking down with love*". Because God sees everything and He has a good memory.

Balance Defined (Though Often Denied)

When it comes to defining balance in the life of a doctoral student, one should not expect distribution of 50% for life and 50% for work. I knew that I have a work-life balance when I can enjoy things that I am doing, whether it doing work-related stuff (duties as a graduate assistant, research, classes, etc.) or recreational/personal activities. With that said, I do not assume that what works for me would work for everyone; what balance is to me might not be a balance for others. If I have to define it, balance means feeling at peace and happy; and that means do the best I can and stop worrying about things (somehow they will fall into place).

Taking Care of Life

I would say I almost never forget to eat, hence, my physical need to survive is taken care of; whereas my spiritual need often forgotten or set aside. More than five times that I made a promise to myself to go for a retreat knowing that I needed it; then I made excuses just as many times I made the promises. Though not everyone would agrees that we need to religious-related activities in order to satisfy our soul or spiritual need; still, there might be more people who would agree that the spiritual part of you needs to be taken care of, regardless of how you would do that. Something to bear in mind though, despite our effort to 'feed' this need, as someone once said, "Our soul is larger than we thought, so we might not feel 100% content at all times". And that is alright.

CODA

Yesterday, as I was finishing this chapter, three students of my cohort were hooded. Having been through two graduation ceremonies myself, I used to think it would just be another ceremony. But I was wrong. As I watched them lining up and hooded, I could feel their joyous walk, smile, hug, and handshake. On their face I saw the pride of earning the doctorate degree; a degree that each of them so well-deserved. Seeing them made me wondered if I could have such a moment when the time comes. I hope it will be as blissful as theirs, I hope it will be the moment where I will say, *"It's worth it!"* instead of *"How much I've given up for this!"*. And I think one way to realize it is by making time for a little bit of everything and with every person that has made a difference in my life.

REFERENCES

Dr. Seuss. (1990). *Oh, The places you'll go!* New York (p. 40), NY: Random House.
U.S. Census Bureau. (2013). *Educational attainment in the United States.* Retrieved from https://www.census.gov/hhes/socdemo/education/data/cps/2013/tables.html

CHAPTER 17

USING THE SKILLS AT THE ECOLOGIES TO BALANCE WORK, HOME, AND SCHOOL AS A DOCTORAL STUDENT

Dagoberto Eli Ramirez

In January 2010, I—as a Hispanic 53-year-old male, husband, father of three, and a Social Studies Coordinator of a large school district with 25 schools and 30,000-plus students at the time—decided to finally apply for admission to the educational leadership doctorate program at the University of Texas-Pan American. I had been thinking and rethinking about it since receiving my masters in educational leadership in 2002, but had talked myself out of it year after year, mostly for fear of the potential difficulty of balancing graduate school with work and family. I forged ahead with the application, got officially accepted in March 2010, and stepped into my first semester that August. As had been predicted, it proved to not be easy. At least once a semester I wanted to quit. I had to remind myself of what I had read when I first entertained the idea of possibly applying for the program—*individuals who apply for doctoral programs are already busy people*. Every time I wanted to quit, I remembered that part of the narrative in the online application packet that stated that. I knew what I was getting into, because

Beyond the Pride and the Privilege: The Stories of Doctoral Students and Work-Life Balance, pages 111–117.

they knew what I was getting into. It was right there in the application packet. It stuck with me from that January 2010 pre-dawn morning when I read it and it in many ways helped me frame and reframe my experiences in the program as I struggled to stick with it day after day, assignment after assignment, semester after semester. I graduated May 2013 only because along the way I learned to harness the necessary technical, political, cultural resources, and leadership skills (Trueba, 1999; Mehan, 2008) at the self, organizational, and community levels (Guajardo, Guajardo, Oliver, Valadez, Keawe, Henderson, & Rocha, 2013) in order to balance life and successfully complete my educational leadership doctoral degree in two and a half years.

The Guajardo et al. (2013) "ecologies of knowing" model has three levels of knowing, namely, the *self*, the *organization*, and the *community*. Guajardo et al. (2013) explained that interactions occur at these three levels to organize conversations, identify entry points, and find spaces for interventions; these ecologies of knowing start at the inner *self*, and then flow out toward the immediate *organization* and subsequently the larger *community*, in a three-ringed concentric circle formation. My life as a doctoral student ebbed and flowed amongst these three ecologies, as I too operated at the *self*, *organization*, and *community* levels, balancing all three realms. As I did so, I also tapped into the *technical*, *political*, and *cultural* leadership skills that Trueba (1999) and Mehan (2008) discussed as being necessary in organizational change and reform. I counted on these leadership skills to maneuver through the challenges I had committed to in the doctoral program. While the Guajardo et al. (2013) "ecologies of knowing" and the leadership skills from Trueba (1999) and Mehan (2008) are models developed to analyze and discuss work that schools do—educational leadership—these frameworks work well here, too, in reframing, reconstructing, and retelling those stories that surface when reflexivity about the lived experiences is allowed. In creating these self-examination narratives, first, I will describe a specific "ecology of knowing" (Guajardo et al., 2013). Next, I will explain which particular Trueba (1999) and Mehan (2008) leadership skills—*technical*, *political*, and *cultural*—connect to that specific "ecology of knowing" (Guajardo et al., 2013) in my work, home, and school life, via stories that best exemplify cross-pollinated experience, illustrating the delicate balancing act.

The most intimate ecology of knowing (Guajardo et al., 2013) is the *self*, where conversations and experiences are made personal and relevant, as it is an opportunity for me as an individual to own my learning and my teaching through story telling; it makes the process personal and gives me an immediate license to act on my own stories. The *technical skills* that Trueba (1999) and Mehan (2008) talked about are those mechanistic tools that leaders implement as a set of preselected skills and strategies to fix issues that arise—the *technician* aspect of leadership. My *technical self* was the side of me in the doctoral process that had to get organized in the balancing act. I knew that in order for me to remain sane, I had to know what was due when and how it needed to be done. I craved for details in every step of the route. I created and depended heavily on color-coded calendars and charts that depicted where I had to be on what day, what was due, and any details that informed the image I needed in order to ensure that that particular event was not undermined. This caused many problems at home, with my wife and children. Near the end of the first semester I was getting moody and downright difficult to put up with, and my wife let me know. "That calendar may run *your* life, but it does not run ours."

While the *technical self* helped balance my work, home, and school, like a mental fulcrum that reminded me that all three prongs had to be balanced, it was at the *organization* level of the ecologies of knowing where the balancing act left the solo arena and truly became a set of relationship projects at work, at home, and at school. As Guajardo et al. (2013) explained, the *organizational* level is critical for learning, as we develop our values, habits, and views of the world; and even at age 53, I was still creating new perspective of those values, habits, and world views. This social view was defined by my interactions with those at work, home, and school; those interactions are most tied in to the *political* and *cultural* leadership skills that Trueba (1999) and Mehan (2008) discussed. Mehan (2008) explained that leading with *political* skills involved working to build productive relationships, galvanizing important political constituencies, while Trueba (1999) shared that *political* clarity was needed in order to harness the asymmetrical power relationships that arise and often remain unchecked otherwise. I quickly learned to use my *political* skills at the *organization* ecology of knowing at all three distinct "organizations"—workplace, school, and home. At work I tapped into those giants who had blazed the trails before me, those recently minted doctors of education at my district—the superintendent, an assistant superintendent, the federal programs director, a federal grant coordinator, and a campus principal. These five doctors became my filters for queries and concerns I had. They shared their stories with me and that proved to be immeasurably useful.

My *political organization* balancing aspect at work started with my superintendent, a very experienced local female who had been part of the very first cohort at my university to go through the doctoral educational leadership program in the early 2000's. Knowing that she herself had been the beneficiary of her own balancing act—wife and mother, school administrator, and doctoral student—in a school system that allowed and supported it, she also allowed me and three other district-wide doctoral candidate colleagues (*and* scores of masters level students) to present a plan of action weekly schedule where we committed to attend university classes and still work the 40-hour work week our contract called for. She could have simply broken my (and my colleagues') dreams to pursue a doctoral degree at the onset, and could have easily justified such action by reminding me that I needed to be focused on my work because in the new era of state testing and accountability, etc., there was no time for anything else. But she chose to support, and quite frankly, even encourage it. This is the *political organization* in the workplace at its very best, looking for opportunities and solutions to challenges. Had the *political organization* winds blown in against me, via some superintendent gale or zephyr, I would have had to either move to another job, or quit school. "All I ask is that you don't neglect your work, *or* your family," she once told me. Once I knew she sanctioned my doctoral degree plans, I enlisted the help of the other new education doctors in the school system. Each one soon made it clear that they too had stood on the shoulders of others ahead of them, though not necessarily in the district. While some *did* point at the same superintendent for leadership and support in their doctoral experiences, most pointed at new-found powerful and power-filled relationships they quickly forged—at school.

The opportunity to live within the *political organization* that the university venue provided proved invaluable, as my doctoral colleagues and I created, established, and developed relationships through which we harnessed our resources together to then forge values, habits, and views of the world (Guajardo et al., 2013); our world, in this case, was the doctoral experience. Beyond the typical group projects that each of my three Fall, three Spring, two Summer I, and two Summer II semesters brought—which *forced* us to work with people we either did not know, nor to whom we naturally gravitated towards—we quickly bought into the notion that we *were* in this together, and we *could* depend on one another to get through both short-term due dates and long-term goals. I was part of Cohort 7, an interesting group of 13 individuals from assorted background—campus principals, assistant principals, and administrators from traditional and charter public schools; central office coordinators, directors, assistant superintendents, and superintendents; and, an unemployed former teacher/tutor/statistician for a national non-profit educational organization who was currently doing stand-up in local venues using "Sexy" as the first part of his stage moniker. Cell and work phone numbers as well as personal e-mail addresses were quickly exchanged as the first two cohort classes in Fall 2010 semester began. While we knew that *getting in* to the program was competitive (as only half of the applicants made it through both the on-line application and in-person assessment center processes), we also sensed that *staying in* was going to be more of a collaborative effort, both academically and affectively. For an initial large group assignment, six of my colleagues became the Six Pack, while I became part of the Super Seven. Some bonds established in that one project have lasted to today. There were weekend meetings at each other's worksites and homes, late night and early morning on-line board posting conversations. Some things, however, did change.

The first two semesters Cohort 7 remained pretty much intact, as all 13 members registered, attended classes, and completed our 12 hours via two classes per semester; I, however, opted to begin to take an additional third class each semester, in essence, getting ahead of my cohort. It proved to be an excellent *political organization* move on my part, for not only did I begin to forge resources-harnessing relationships with new colleagues who were in previous cohorts, I began to establish deeper more intimate connections with my professors. In retrospect, I believe the professors saw it as proof of just how serious I was about being able to effectively balance home, work, and school, no matter if I increased the expected school-load by 50 percent. I remember feeling like a fish out of water in the first extra class that first semester, joining five students who were either getting ready to take their comps, or develop and defend their research proposal—I was an old newbie in the midst of experienced younger vets. I sat, listened, participated, and was in awe of their calm expertise as I tried to learn as much from them as I could. I also quickly began to try to zero-in on what my *possible* research topic, problem questions, etc. *might* be—already, in my *first* semester. Our professor began every "Hispanics in Education" topical seminar session by asking one of us, "Okay, so-and-so, so what is *your* problem?!" I went from it initially taking me aback to my subsequently looking forward to the professional banter around potential research directions in which we were all separately heading. As hectic as this load-and-a-half that I signed up for was—and as further trickier balancing home, work, school all became—this deep immersion I chose to put myself into actually created a more solid and more serious commitment to finish what I had started. I was all in.

While I added more to my balancing plate, some of my Cohort 7 colleagues began to struggle with keeping up. The drift-away began in both summer semesters that ended our year one, as some cohort members opted to take the summer off; they essentially fell two semesters behind, for each summer session was a fast-paced regular two-course six-hour semester. At the end of my full year one, I was still happily married with three connected children, I was still running the social studies program for my large district of 25 campuses and 30,000+ students, *and* I had successfully balanced my way to my first 30 hours of the 69-hour doctoral educational leadership program as I eagerly signed up for my first 9 hours of year two. My summer-off colleagues started their year two with 12 hours, and were now having to figure out how they were going to play catch-up in future semesters, possibly with the *new* Cohort 8 that had just started. The *political organization* reality and work at school had come together for me. But the *political organization* realms were not restricted to the two prongs of work and school, for the home *is* also an organization and there are important home politics that cannot and should not be ignored. The relationships at home by their very nature involve more intimacy, familiarity, and close continuous physical proximity, as we always start and end the day in the same set of rooms in the same building; so, it is no surprise that it was the politics at home that both cushioned and fueled the challenges that being heavily busy with three separate full-time realities engendered. Although my wife is a teacher/counselor and has been through many educational rodeos with me, still, her signing up to go on *this* ride required a constant reminder from me to her that always seemed to start with, "Didn't we agree…?" We had.

That particular recurring rejoinder from me to my wife began to emerge as the excitement of the novelty of my joining the doctoral program began to wear thin, and maybe even wear off completely. Just as I could only claim once, or *maybe* twice in that first extra class—the "Hispanics in Education" topical seminar—that

I was *new* at this and get some empathy from my veteran classmates and the professor, my "Honey, but don't you see what I'm going through?!" at home with my wife only worked a few times that first Fall semester. Then it became an old hat, and then she reminded me that I had volunteered for this experience. The home *political organization* format that immediately began to evolve became in the end an agreed-to arrangement of a three-year series of long working days, short sleepy-nights, no non-work weekends, and many, many, *many* missed family things of one sort or another. But through all this, the home *political organization* dynamics proved to be the most important to both harness and juggle. While my wife truly understood way in advance of me applying what a commitment of time and space this would entail from all in the family, and while my three children were not tiny babies anymore (a daughter teaching, a daughter at UT Austin, and my son in high school and at the community college), life sometimes *just happened.* And it always seemed to *just happen* at those key most "inopportune moments" when several heavy reading assignments were being read, or when some large project was being planned. But, in retrospect, when does life *not* happen that way? In the middle of my second year my 80-year-old father became bedridden and non-communicatively ill. When he was in his last days, I sat through two weeks of classes where I had to explain to my professors that I had to have my cell phone on because…

The night Dad died I did not first call or text my boss at work, or my two Teaching American History grant coordinators and grant specialist who worked under me, nor my wonderful secretary who greased my office's wheels and kept me organized. As important as they were to me, the first non-family members that I reached out when that part of life—death—happened, were my professors and my doctoral candidate colleagues. My wife knew that although someday school would all end, they were now extended family. Looking back, during that crucial second year in the program, when I was racing forward and others were slowing back down, the *political organization* connections that became almost just as important to me as my wife and three children were not my work buddies—some whom I had known for decades—but rather my professors whom I was getting closer to and my school mates who were with me in the same arena. I had researched and had helped prepare a triad presentation the days prior, and was getting ready to attend class that evening when the call came from my brother, that it was time to implement the "do not resuscitate order" that our family had come to consensus on months before. My classmates presented without me, and I knew that not only were they going to be fine without me, I was going to be fine with them and my professor. The *political organization* relationships our cohort developed those two initial years united us not only as classmates in a rigorous doctoral program, but as human beings connected by life's most intimate experiences; during my program years, our cohort celebrated and suffered together, births and deaths, weddings and divorces, family coming home and moving away.

In a sense, as old as we all were—with at least two degrees under our belts—we all grew up balancing our lives together.

At the third level of the "ecologies of knowing," Guajardo et al. (2013) explained that it is at the *community* level that we learn the skills, build the awareness, and plan the actions to change the behaviors and narratives in order to create the new politic informed by caring and sustaining the quality of life for every child and every citizen. This is guided by *cultural* leadership skills that help engage our values, belief systems, and norms (Mehan, 2008). Thus, the ethical and moral compass of my balancing act was established by my *cultural community* conscience which found its way into my final project—my dissertation research aptly named "Case Study of a School District's Implementation of a Culturally Relevant Social Studies Curriculum." Even way back in semester one, when my topical seminar professor asked "And what *is* your problem?" I knew I wanted to invest my research and dissertation time researching, writing about, and advocating for a *cultural community* topic that would potentially make a difference in the educational community in which I was born and which I was still serving. Part of the necessary balancing work between home, work, and school had to be informed by this overarching metaphysical query: "What does this all matter in this big scheme of life?" The answer to that philosophical inquiry is grounded on the premise that the balancing work that I had to do in order to successfully accomplish the goal of completing my doctoral experience—and not become part of the group that does *not* finish—was part of an intricate web of resources that I had learned to harness during those 53 years before applying to the program. It serves as a balancing model. It matters because I have proof, yet again, that accessing technical, political, and cultural resources and leadership skills at the self, organizational, and community levels makes all the difference in balancing home, work, and school.

REFERENCES

Guajardo. M., Guajardo, F., Oliver, J., Valadez, M. M., Keawe, L. O., Henderson, K., & Rocha, P. (2013). Part 3: Reframing the political imagination: Stories of advocacy from educational leaders. *University Council for Educational Administration Review, 54*(1), 30–33.

Mehan, H. (2008). Engaging the sociological imagination: My journey into design research and public sociology. *Anthropology & Education Quarterly, 39*(1), 77–91.

Trueba, H.T. (1999). *Latinos unidos: From cultural diversity to the politics of solidarity.* New York, NY: Rowman& Littlefield Publishers, Inc.

CHAPTER 18

SOARING ON THE WINGS OF SANKOFA

Ethnographical Retrospective of a Black Woman Pursuing the PhD

Juhanna Rogers

The Sankofa bird is a folkloric bird that is often used to reference the past of African peoples. Sankofa birds fly forward just like any other bird; however, its unique characteristic is that while flying forward its head is turned backwards. The Sankofa symbolizes the importance of looking back while moving forward; never forgetting where you come from. I cannot recall where I first learned about the Sankofa or who told me the story; however, the meaning and symbolism sticks. As a young girl, I always wanted to see the world. I wanted to travel the globe to learn about cultures and language as a performance artist. However, that dream turned into working in higher education creating international programs for urban students of color. No matter where I am in the world, I am constantly reflecting the journey of my ancestors, particularly the women, who endured the horrors of America's racial and gendered past, migrated and fought for an education in so that I have opportunities they did not. As a doctoral student it is on their shoulders that I stand. Therefore, figuring out how to manage my personal life and

Beyond the Pride and the Privilege: The Stories of Doctoral Students and Work-Life Balance, pages 119–125.

professional life is critical to, not just my success, but to the success of those who follow me. Since childhood a community of Black elders sowed into me the importance of knowing the struggles and histories of Black America and the strides made, despite barriers placed before them. Through the teachings bestowed upon me by elders, I acquired skills and knowledge that have taken me far beyond my expectations. Growing up, almost every woman I knew was a matriarch and in their own way activists in the Black community. These women, in addition to working fulltime, were entrepreneurs, leaders in the church, staff members in after-school programs, and girl scout troop leaders. They not only took a stake in raising their children, they were passionate about instilling positive values in the children within their communities.

In 2005, I left the home community, of Newark, NJ and moved across country to Indianapolis to pursue my master's in higher education. My son was three months old. My grandmother and mother were highly concerned about my ability to manage a newborn, the demands of graduate school, and life in a new city. Working and going to school with a newborn was quite a task and leaving my home and support system to do so was a major risk. I completed my masters in 2007 and went to work for the same university. In 2010, I realized that my passion was beyond being an advocate for African American students as a staff member; I wanted to research issues of race and racism at predominantly white institutions and design international academic programs that would increase the participation of Black students in study abroad. Therefore, I reorganized my life and resigned from my job during one of the worst economic downturns in American history. However, I started an educational consultant company that created and directed international programs and began the journey to the PhD. Today, I am in my final year of coursework.

As a doctoral student, I find myself battling to maintain the characteristics of the women from my community without failing and fighting this battle is not easy. What made me stop and re-evaluate my ability to engage the community and excel in the academy was my health. In late December of 2011, I had developed acidities of the stomach and spent about 4 months learning how to eat again so that I would not be sick and in pain. I was baffled by this condition because I had never had stomach problems or concerns prior to graduate school. My doctor indicated that this problem is seen often in patients that are in high-stress environments and with poor diets. Between doctor visits and repeated episodes, I spent a lot of time over the next year thinking about my academic work, goals, schedule, and how it influenced my diet, time, and personal relationships. This narrative explores how an African American mother/doctoral student finds balance.

MY STORY

I became a mom a year after completing undergrad; I was 23 years old. When I learned I was pregnant it became urgent that I pursue this dream. Becoming a mother forced me to consider other options because I wanted to show my son that working should be something that enhances your well-being in addition to providing financial support for your family. My son, even before he was born, challenged me to focus on where it is that I wanted to go. Eight years later, life has taken me on quite the journey.

It was the fall of 2011 and my son had just started first grade. I was in my second year of the program. I was taking a full course-load for the first time on the Bloomington campus. Taking classes in Bloomington required me to commute two and a half hours, roundtrip, three days a week. In addition, I was a research associate 20 hours a week, teaching an online class, presenting at conferences, completing class assignments, all while trying to keep my son involved in athletics on weekends. Coffee, which I had never drunk before, became a morning, afternoon, and evening staple, which led to me being hospitalized shortly after handing in my last paper.

A year later, my stomach is better; I still have to watch my diet and I am learning more about healthy ways to eat. However, this experience made it very evident that I needed to re-evaluate the way I was going about my work and managing my responsibilities. I identified several factors that my support network was lacking in terms of personal and social support that comes with living in an unfamiliar place or near family. This brought me back to the essence of the Sankofa bird and the women I watched as a young girl. I began to ask myself, "How did they manage work, family, and self?" I often left the latter, self, out of the equation. My health began to suffer because I was constantly in battle with finding time for the things I love and the demands associated with doctoral study.

Most of my day is spent addressing someone's needs or expectation. Between my mommy's calls about the latest sales at a local store, my son's teachers and coaches emailing about assignments and practices, and my professors', and students' modifications and updates, I am usually exhausted by 1 p.m. I must prioritize who to respond to, which assignments to begin first, and who I can send to voicemail, or respond to a later time. Additionally, as a full-time student my assistantship, which pays my tuition and provides income, has its role to be filled.

Working on the PhD requires a bit of selfishness, which causes tension between completing an academic task and fulfilling the social and cultural demands of being a mother, daughter, and sister. It seemed the stress became more intense because no matter what I choose to do, I missed out on something or someone. If I put my family and students first then I was angry because my coursework would suffer. If I did course work first, it required me to work alone blocking the rest of world out because isolation is necessary when reading, writing, and analyzing right? I was plagued with guilt and frustration; this is a burden that I bare. During down times of the year, summer and winter breaks, I planned family trips home and to visit my grandmother to preserve my sanity.

I am a Black African American female, first generation college graduate - master's degree holder, a mother, a daughter, a sister, an entrepreneur, a doctoral student, and adjunct faculty. In addition, my ethnic and cultural roles and responsibilities permeate my academic self. Maintaining the role of student, teacher, professional, daughter, and mother is not a short task. At any given moment of the day several people will call upon me to fulfill a request, need, or demand. Each of these identities is critical and relevant to my experience as a doctoral student. As I enter the final stages of my doctoral course work, I needed to decide which of these roles is most important and then seek answers on how I would balance it all?!. Glidersleeve et al. (2011) asks a question that I have asked myself several times, "Am I going crazy?" I too have struggled with this same question, While affirming and validating my experiences being true to who I am.

Seeking Salience in Familiar Space

Recently, I attended the National Council for Negro Women Annual Black History Luncheon. I was provided a ticket by my mentor and sat at her table amongst friends. I hadn't seen her in months and this provided us an opportunity to reconnect and catch up on my life events and research progress. At this point in time, I was spending a lot of time trying to juggle multiple responsibilities to meet deadlines, demands, and expectations. I asked my mentor how she juggled these things, since she was a mother and doctoral student at one time. She told me, "First, Juhanna, you need to stop trying to juggle things. Juggling means you are not prioritizing based on what is most important. You need to choose what is more important to you and do those things first and be satisfied with what you achieve."

My mentor's (the godmother of campus) words penetrated my mind and heart. Moving from juggling to prioritizing demanded that I re-evaluate who I am, and determine who I wanted to become. Having a clear indication of that would help me prioritize. So at the age of 30, I found myself creating a list of my identities and the roles I played in life. I also listed the tasks and responsibilities, professionally, personally, and academically that went along with my roles and identities.

While pondering my balance strategies, I thought back to the women of my childhood. Understanding of what it means to be an African American woman, mother, and doctoral student results in my mental, spiritual, and emotional states being constantly in flux. I had to learn how to manage tasks, roles, responsibilities, and emotions that go along with each of my identities. Balancing all of the roles and responsibilities that come with motherhood, being a doctoral student, and young Black woman constantly require me to return to my roots and experiences with my elders to help guide me.

Good mentorship, establishing a support network, and the significance in doing work that I am passionate about. All helped. I completed a master's in Higher Education in 2007 and worked for two and half years at a predominantly White urban campus in Indianapolis. Instrumental to my success was a group of African American female mentors, administrators, faculty and staff, that helped me adjust. Almost all of them had raised children while completing graduate school. These other mothers were a shoulder of support, helped find me local resources, and offered professional development opportunities. It is with their wisdom and guidance that I remain humbled and certain that despite my challenges I can get through this.

After identifying the roles and identities that affected my daily life, I realized that while the course work is a challenge, the doctoral socialization process is what has had the most strenuous effect on my life. The process required more than mentorship, a vow of poverty, and determination; it is a process that requires you to think strategically about how to organize and connect work to people, places, and topics. The environment is filled with arrogance and politics that left me questioning my potential and place on days when I can't seem to finish a project, return my mother's phone call, and read articles on top of attending my son's game. I am constantly up against a clock, deadlines, and personal demands. As a result my health suffered.

I developed a bad stomach due to high stress levels and poor diet while going through this process. However, prioritizing has helped me say, "Screw it. I have to make sacrifices or I will miss out on what's really most important—making sure my son is loved and cared for and knows that he is more important than any degree." Secondly, I decided that I needed time to be me and do social things within the community for two reasons, because I needed to relax and enjoy myself and because the community around me needed help too. Ultimately, I found that family time and community engagement were central to the development of my work as a scholar.

Establishing Priorities: Guideposts to Work Life Balance

Collins (1999), author of *Black Feminist Thought*, describes the role of Black women and the ways they manage the multiple demands of their roles, historically and presently, as a form of resistance. Black female resistance is often overlooked and minimized. Collins argues that throughout history our images, stories, and bodies have been co-opted, sold or undervalued by dominant society around the globe. I recommend that other Black women and mothers, pursing the doctorate, consider the historical forms of resistance that Black women have used.

As a Black woman from a working class family, the demands of my life and my experiences are deeply connected to the historical struggles of being Black in America. My culture, race, gender, and socio-economic status directly affect my experience as a doctoral student. Subsequently, I work multiple jobs in order to provide for my family while pursuing my terminal degree. My day to day circumstances are connected to the oppressive economic structures that have affected working class people of color for decades. There were times when my financial status and demands of this program almost made me quit; however, in the back of my mind the images of my ancestors and those who came before me entered my mind.

My African American female mentors and my community of elders from childhood reminded me to assess my priorities. Over the last five years, my relationship to my African American elders and mentors motivated and influenced the direction of my research, my values as a woman, mother, and scholar. Based on this understanding, I offer a few recommendations to other daughters, mothers, sisters, and women who are trying to find balance.

The doctoral socialization process requires doctoral students who aim to become faculty to write, publish, take classes, present, serve on committees, work in isolation, focus, multitask, be mentored, be innovative, humble, and confident. As an African American woman, these demands conflicted with my worldviews. Therefore, instead of just adopting characteristics associated with the socialization process, I developed a method that helped me remain true to myself while meeting the goals and expectations set before me. For example, when assigned course material doesn't cover literature dealing with the Black experience, I found some and introduced them to the class during discussions. In addition, I centered my research on race, racism, and gender; I began to use Critical Race Theory (CRT) in my research.

Through CRT, I recognize what is happening to me is not just happenstance or due to lack of preparation. My struggles in the academy were connected to the historical struggle of Black people; we strive to achieve more for the sake of their family and community. Exploring the racialized experiences of Blacks in the academy took more time because I had to find the literature, identify scholars who give voice to marginalized groups, and then connect it back to theory. For example, when in the history of higher education class I chose to read *History of Black Women in the Ivory Tower* (Evans, 2007), I was reminded that the challenges that I face do not define me, and despite various roles I manage, I am confident that I, too, can make it. CRT allowed me to keep my priorities as my goals. A well known CRT scholar of urban education at an American Education Research Association conference told me, "Research on race is not always easy and readily available. It requires knowledge of interdisciplinary literature and scholars. Depending on the assignment, you may have to consult sociological or historical sources that may not be introduced in class." This senior scholar brought me comfort by acknowledging the work I aimed to do was needed and that he and others were working to lay the foundation. In addition, connecting my experiences or the experiences of other African Americans to my research alleviates some of the burden of being away from home at times because the projects are connected to people I care about. For example, I submitted papers to my son's school or teachers to help address inequalities, or I discussed the topic with my family and friends, which includes them in the experience. I strove to keep my family connected to this work is by letting my friends and family read my work. A prime example is I let my brother and my friends read this book chapter to provide feedback about the authenticity of my story. Incorporating the community and my loved ones has helped eliminate the guilt and frustration that can come with working in isolation.

By prioritizing and defining myself for myself, personally and academically, I discovered part of my pitfalls were due in part to the notion that I had to be their definition of great. Being caught up in the pursuit of the doctorate, I believed that I was supposed to be excellent at writing, research, grant writing, and presenting.

I accepted advice given to me by my advisor and academic mother, "Do what I am good at and work collaboratively with others to improve what you're not." When I think about my research projects and work in the Black community there was always a group who worked to make progress. Martin Luther King, Malcolm X, Bethune Cookman, Julia Ann Cooper, and many other leaders worked with others. Maybe that was why there was a team of mothers doing community activities when I was young?! I recognized that I can't do everything in one day. Some experiences, deadlines, and tasks would have to wait for another time; I had to debunk the superwomen myth and begin to say, "No, I can't serve on that committee," "Yes, I do need help," or, "I will send you a tentative timeline on that because I am working on another project at the moment." Today, not only am I healthier, but I am certain about the scholar I am becoming. I recommend more women of color take the time to examine themselves as a part of the research process. Research became a sense of therapy. In the last year of my course work, my health improved tremendously. I was in a better state of mind because I focused in uncovering narratives and highlighting the experiences of Blacks in education, collaborated with other Black women, and owned my priorities and limitation. The collaboration with other women colleagues going through the program with me, was instrumental and critical to my development.

Flying on Forward

My decision to pursue a PhD is a testimony to those who fought to survive in a racially and gendered America. It is on the back of these courageous women that I stand and sit as I write, read, analyze, re-read, re-write, in order to bring voice to the Black educational experience. Collins (1999) describes the role of Black women and the way they manage the multiple demands of their roles, as a form of resistance to the White male dominant society. The journey to the professoriate is a work of resistance (Collins, 1999), formal and informal. As a woman of color, I am reminded daily through blatant and subtle interactions, that the academy was not designed with me and my community values in mind; nonetheless, I am learning to resist because earning the PhD is a way to serve the community I left behind. In these short pages I tell a piece of my story with hopes that another sister can find comfort in knowing that she is not alone. Just like the women and men who have gone before us, we may ponder whether you are capable, ready, smart enough, or going crazy at times; however, if you take a minute and reflect back on whence we came maybe you can see, "You, too, are flying on the wings of a Sankofa".

REFERENCES

Collins, P. H. (1999). *Black feminist thought: Knowledge, consciousness, and the politics of empowerment.* Routledge.

Evans, S. Y. (2007). *Black women in the ivory tower, 1850–1954.* Gainesville, FL: University Press of Florida.

CHAPTER 19

WRITE, RUN, REPEAT

A Rewarding Marathon to the Phd and Wellness

Leslie Jo Shelton

I am currently a full-time doctoral candidate in a higher education administration program. I am also a runner, yogi, weight lifter, and overall workout enthusiast, but this only came about a few years ago. Originally from the Midwest, I am a first-generation college student who was raised by my mother. As a kid, I was a dancer and later a high school volleyball player who sustained myself on whatever typical teenage junk food was lying around the house. I maintained my love of sports during college where I also became a vegetarian for political and spiritual reasons. Throughout my undergraduate and master's programs, I held live-in staff positions that provided on-campus meal plans, so I never learned to cook healthy vegetarian meals for myself because plenty of options were offered in the campus dining halls. During my master's program in student affairs I sustained a traumatic ankle injury in an intramural softball game. This injury left me unable to walk fully for about six months and resulted in a long period of physical inactivity that eventually became an unhealthy pattern I sustained over time.

Fast-forward to four years ago when I left a full-time Student Affairs administration position in the Southwest to move across country and become a doctoral student. Throughout this transition, I was met with extremely supportive

Beyond the Pride and the Privilege: The Stories of Doctoral Students and Work-Life Balance, pages 127–131.

and welcoming faculty at my new institution and a wonderful network of students in our program. Despite finding myself in a great new community of scholars, I still faced a significant struggle in my transition. Limited resources such as time, money, and energy influenced my ability to balance school/work opportunities and to maintain a healthy lifestyle.

I am fortunate to be a part of a PhD program with many wonderful possibilities for involvement outside of the classroom. I enjoy the flexibility and autonomy associated with these opportunities, but the ambiguous nature of this graduate student lifestyle led to imbalance; I channeled my resources into work and neglected my health. With no clearly defined "end" to work, I did a poor job of self-regulating my level of life balance. I dedicated my time and energy primarily to academics and maintaining a social life, while closely budgeting my graduate student income. I did not realize how my health would suffer if I did not make time to work out or to learn to shop for and cook healthy foods. Also, I was unsure how to choose an affordable workout facility or shop for healthy, yet affordable groceries. Before I realized it, my initial adjustment as a full time PhD student became a longer-term pattern of sacrificing my personal health to accomplish my school/work goals.

As an eager new doctoral student, I anticipated jumping into exciting work and school activities full-force, especially as I did not have family responsibilities competing for my time and energy. Of course, I still had important relationships in life to nurture, but none that required me to be in a primary caregiver role. Many of my loved ones were close friends who also worked in Student Affairs or were also graduate students, so they understood my efforts at balancing personal relationships with school and work. This personal support afforded me a great chance to immerse myself in many things my academic program and institution had to offer including teaching, serving in assistantships, working in additional campus positions, and conducting research abroad. During these activities, surrounded by my new chosen family, I felt very well adjusted to my role as a full-time PhD student.

Despite feeling content with the academic and social aspects of my new life, I developed harmful personal habits regarding my health. For example, after long days of meetings, teaching, attending class, and working on research, I did not find it appealing to leave home again for a workout, only to return to shop for fresh groceries and then to cook a healthy meal. Instead, I wanted to watch reruns of Grey's Anatomy and order a pizza while sitting on my futon in my snuggie. Even though this could have been occasional rewarding downtime away from schoolwork, I did not leave these quiet moments feeling refreshed or recharged; instead I felt drained of energy. Despite having incredible experiences and being surrounded by supportive people, by January of my second year, I realized I was neglecting my health.

A few events during my second year of the program culminated in a lifestyle change where I began to emphasize health in my work-life balance. The day after returning from a summer of research abroad, I had an interview for an hourly campus position. I dug into my closet to discover that two months of dining on local fare like poutine, combined with not exercising routinely, had resulted in my professional wardrobe feeling more than snug. I attended the interview in my "schmedium" button-up shirt and did not think about this surprising wardrobe fail too much after that day. In the following months, I kept getting colds that would not go away and were negatively impacting my work productivity. The fall of my second year, a routine cold virus turned into a month and a half of illness that caused me to miss a professional conference I was really excited about. My energy level and immune system were suffering from a year and a half of poor nutrition and infrequent physical activity. Sitting in classes or meetings and working at my laptop for long hours was also taking a toll on my health, and I ended up in the campus health center physical therapy clinic for some neck and back concerns. During this time, I realized that I was not alone in neglecting my health since starting my PhD.

Despite encountering health challenges, there were many wonderful aspects of my academic program, including the community of scholars that extends beyond our classrooms. Peers spanning over the cohort years have become dear friends who also provide one other a great deal of support. I began to notice that several of us were consistently commenting on how our lives had changed since starting the PhD program. We were in agreement that we felt extremely happy in our program and were so fortunate to be a part of such an amazing academic community. However, we commiserated over feeling like schoolwork had taken over our lives, resulting in being unhealthy and the most out of shape we have ever been.

In addition to an overall unhealthy lifestyle shift, certain times in the academic program are known for being particularly stressful and difficult to navigate while maintaining balance. For example, there are (true!) legends of second year students who survived comprehensive exams by not sleeping or showering for over four days straight, while surviving on a diet of Twizzlers and cheesy poofs. These realities were put into further perspective when I began seeing my peers in the campus physical therapy office. The medical professionals there explained that graduate students are their number one clients due to unhealthy habits developed like sitting for hours, neglecting physical activity, and poor nutrition. Were these doctors essentially telling me that getting a PhD was hazardous to our health?! As my grad student friends and I like to say, "This was NOT in the brochure!"

By the end of my second fall semester, I had a final "ah-ha!" moment when I saw a picture I took with some cohort friends and I barely recognized myself. Reality set in. This surprising photo was a reflection of me being unhealthy despite feeling fulfilled in other areas of my life. I was so excited to get up each day and be a part of a field and academic program I loved, but I needed to ensure that I was taking care of myself so I could be around to enjoy this work for many years to come. It occurred to me that I needed to do something to channel as much energy and passion into my personal well being as I did towards my work and school. I also realized that I was not serving as an effective role model for my students.

At the time, I was teaching an undergraduate leadership class and I worked with students on their holistic development both in and outside of the classroom. It became clear I was not engaging in the same self-care that I encouraged my students to practice.

Similarly, as an aspiring faculty member, I wanted to practice healthy life habits during my PhD so I could model balance for the graduate students I hoped to mentor in the future. I also wanted to serve as a support and positive example for my cohort peers who had expressed frustration with their work-life balance struggles regarding health. Graduate school is a time of limited resources, including scarce time, money, and energy outside of activities directly related to schoolwork. However, I realized there was no time like the present to reprioritize and develop healthy habits that would ultimately increase my enjoyment in all aspects of life for many years to come. So, I woke up one January day and decided to embark on a journey to join my peers in some creative and fun ways to begin our quest for health and balance. This decision would lead to me finding a renewed love for sports and fitness, including a new hobby of running - something I never would have considered possible for me to engage in and enjoy.

My group of amazing colleagues and friends initiated many successful ideas that have helped us make budget-friendly healthy life choices in staying balanced amidst our hectic graduate student schedules. For example, what started as a "walk and talk" group to power walk through campus while reviewing class materials turned into an open running group that led to accomplishments I never thought possible; I finished my first races, including 5Ks, 10Ks, and several half-marathons. I am certainly not gazelle-like in my running, nor do I train for speed and record setting. However, challenging myself in fun and fitness remain my main running goals, which my friends have supported in many ways including running with me, cheering me on at race finish lines, and joining for post-race celebration brunch. Having the support of my academic family in my running endeavors has been extremely rewarding for me personally and has provided a healthy break from schoolwork. Training for races motivates me to meet my daily work goals so I can hit the pavement later while jamming to my favorite 90s iTunes mix. In addition to the physical benefits of running, it also allows for mental and emotional gains in forming deeper relationships with training buddies while also offering peaceful reflection time in nature during solo runs. Running throughout the area has also given me great joy in getting to know my new home state in an intimate way instead of staying in my campus bubble. Running helped jumpstart my healthy lifestyle change, and other activities have also been central in keeping me excited about maintaining good health as I strive to nurture my body as much as I do my mind through academics.

Running is an important release I look forward to after a long day of schoolwork, and I have found yoga to be the perfect supplement to rejuvenate my spirit too. During our second year, my good cohort friend pulled me into her new fitness routine and was instrumental in connecting me to some of my favorite workout spots in town, including an introduction to yoga class. I remember how nervous I was before our first class. Would I be expected to wear expensive spandex, stand on my head, and reach spiritual enlightenment in a 103 degree room? I also recall how sore we were after our first yoga class, as we had to sit in the car for a long while and have a power smoothie before we could muster the strength to drive home. However, now we are yoga regulars and I cannot imagine my life without this centering time in my week. The ability to connect on my mat and "just be" has been invaluable in bridging the spiritual aspect of my school/work/life connection, especially as I grapple with complex and personal areas of social justice work in my research. Our favorite local yoga studio is donation-based, which fits our graduate student budgets, and has become an important part of our community here, offering our group a peaceful place to decompress outside of school.

In addition to increasing my activity level, investing in an overall healthy lifestyle meant I actually learned to cook and bake, all with limited time and on a grad student budget. As a vegetarian who did not know how to cook, I realized I had turned into a "carb-atarian" with my daily chow of cheese-its, pizza, and campus event leftovers. Thankfully, my best friend in my cohort is also my neighbor and a great cook. She would often make me tasty dishes while patiently explaining how to make these creations. She even offered support many times when I caught things on fire in my oven, dumped blenders full of muffin batter on my head (true story) or got too creative with ingredient substitutions. My friends are certainly good sports, as many of my earlier modified recipe attempts looked, and tasted, like science experiments gone awry. However, learning to make healthy goodies contributed to increasing my healthy nutrition while also being a fun way to share treats with friends who are also looking for nutritious snacks. I still enjoy a processed cheese snack or gooey pizza, but now I also take the time to balance my nutrition with healthy snacks and well-planned meals. I have also benefitted from experiencing how eating healthier helps me perform better in my fitness pursuits. This positive cycle is reaffirming, especially given the support I have from enthusiastic peers who have shared much of this journey with me.

During the past few years, my friends have noticed the physical changes that have occurred for me, but most importantly, I became healthier on the inside. This includes having more energy and focus, which brought a new level of productivity and joy to my work. I always remind myself to "put good in and get good out." For me, this means that focusing on my health does not detract from the time and energy I spend on my studies; instead, leading a holistically healthy lifestyle results in increased energy and enjoyment with my work and a higher quality end product. Overall, the zeal with which I approach my work is now matched with the attention I give to my health. As I enter the final year of my academic program, I remind myself that the perseverance it took to accomplish my health goals also translates to my ability to achieve my academic and professional goals. This is a journey of balance that I look forward to continuing into the future as I work to complete my dissertation and explore new fitness adventures!

CHAPTER 20

MENUDO FOR THE SPIRIT

Marissa Vásquez Urias

I was 16 when I experienced my first heartbreak. As I lay locked up in my room, feeling that my world was coming to an end, a gentle knock on my door brought me back to my senses. It was my mom. She had been by my side all day, wiping my tears and telling me that I would be okay. However, as a young, naïve teenager, I thought to myself, *how could she possibly know how I feel?* Walking in, I saw her place a book on my nightstand. She took my hands in hers and said, "*Mija,* I know that you're going through a difficult time right now. And I know that you may not want to talk to me about it. So I bought you this book. Maybe it'll cheer you up." When she left the room I sat up in my bed and reached over for the book. The title of it was *Chicken Soup for the Teenage Soul.* I skimmed through the table of contents and stopped at the section entitled, "On Relationships." As I began reading, I found myself relating to similar stories of first loves, breakups, and sorrow. The lessons prescribed by each of these narratives involved perseverance, believing in oneself, caring for others, and inner-strength. My mom was right. While I valued her love and support, there was something different about relating to my peers. The more that I read their stories, the stronger I felt about sharing mine.

The complexity of life's challenges have certainly evolved since I was 16, but the value of sharing my failures and successes are what continue to keep me grounded. The continued support from my family and the mentorship that I have

Beyond the Pride and the Privilege: The Stories of Doctoral Students and Work-Life Balance, pages 133–138.

received from fellow scholars and advisors has been instrumental to my persistence. As a Latina doctoral student, I know that my experiences are not unique to those sharing my struggle. However, my hope is that those reading this narrative will find comfort in knowing that this journey is not impossible. ¡Si se Puede![1] And just as *Chicken Soup* re-energized my soul, I hope that the stories in this book serve as the menudo[2] that fuels your spirit.

New Beginnings

"Damn Deedee! Aren't you tired of studying?" This was the response from my sister after telling her of my intent to apply to a doctorate program. While most of my family thought I was crazy for considering another three years of school, the truth was, I missed the intellectual stimulation of being in a classroom. It had been nearly two years since completing my master's program and I had yet to secure a full-time job. As the budget crisis in California continued to escalate, particularly in education, I lost hope of ever achieving my goal of becoming a community college counselor. The economic downturn coupled with the competitiveness for employment within the community college system was disheartening. After months of various consulting gigs with my mentor, Dr. Ken Gonzalez, I was hired as a full-time employee at a non-profit organization. However, while my work at the organization was fulfilling, I longed to return to the community college setting. My passion for higher education, particularly community colleges, stemmed from personal experiences as a transfer student who had been nurtured, both academically and socially, by my *Puente*[3] counselors and instructors. As a *Puentista*, I was challenged to think critically about education, including my own role as a socially conscious Latina. Such empowerment led me to continue my education and inspired me to help others do the same. Thus, I was determined to find a way back to the community college system. Thankfully, with the support of loved ones, I applied to the Educational Leadership Program (EdD) at San Diego State University.

My initial response to my acceptance was that of excitement and anxiousness. I was eager to begin this new chapter in my life, especially as my husband had just completed his first year of law school. Yet, it wasn't long before these emotions subsided and were replaced with thoughts of doubt and uncertainty. As the youngest, least experienced, and only individual not working in a higher education setting in my cohort, I questioned whether I made the right decision to enter into a practitioner-based program. As more of a research/theory kind-of-girl, I became frustrated and bored with my coursework. I came home after every class venting about the lack of intellectual stimulation and the drawn out discussions about APA formatting and how to write in academic prose. My disillusionment with the program prompted disdain and ungratefulness of the opportunity I had been given.

One evening, my husband finally sat me down for an intervention. He told me that since beginning the program, I had become irritable, negative, and unhappy. I was completely taken aback by his comments, though not because I disagreed.

Rather, I was concerned over how such negativity was affecting others in my life. Had I been disrespectful to my parents, co-workers, or other family members? Was I projecting my dissatisfaction with the program in an unprofessional way towards faculty and my classmates? My husband reminded me of the excitement that I once had about joining the program, and of my passion for becoming a change agent within higher education. He was right. As a Latina, I knew that the opportunity to pursue a doctoral degree was one that is not afforded to many women of color. At that moment, I told myself that I would become more proactive in balancing my family, work, school, professional development, and maintaining my sanity!

The Balancing Act

As with most doctoral students, balancing my family life has been a challenge. Although I am a third generation Latina, the traditional cultural value of *familismo* still exists within my family. Many scholars have operationalized and dissected the impact that this cultural notion has on Latino students in education (Marin & Marin, 1991; Ojeda, Navarro, & Morales, 2011; Suarez-Orozco & Suarez-Orozco, 1995; Valenzuela, 1999). In short, it means putting family first, even if it requires sacrificing personal responsibilities or commitments. While I know that my *familia* always has my back, subtle jokes and comments such as, "¡Ya no me quieres, *hija!*" or "I guess I'll see you when I see you," has made it difficult to find a balance between focusing on my studies and spending enough time with family. This is even more challenging coming from a large family, where I often miss out on numerous get-togethers, birthday celebrations, holidays, and other special occasions due to school. Over the years I have endured my share of guilt trips for not calling or visiting enough. This constant battle between upholding my family values and accomplishing my goals is emotionally and psychologically draining. I ask myself, "Am I doing the right thing? Have I misplaced my priorities? Am I being selfish?" Each time I force myself to remember that my sacrifices will pay off in the end. While I don't spend as much time as I would like with my husband and my family, I do what I can to let them know that they are in my thoughts.

Aside from spending most of our evenings and weekends at the library together, my husband and I make time late at night to catch up on our favorite television shows or grab dinner with friends. Throughout the day, we send each other cheesy text messages or Facebook posts as reminders that we are thinking of each other. As for my family, I make it a point to see or speak with my parents at least two or three times a week. This includes visiting their home during my lunch breaks (and raiding their fridge) or calling them as I'm driving from work to school. The long-distance relationship with my sister (who lives in North Carolina) is maintained through weekly Skype calls or silly Snapchat messages. As cliché as it sounds, it's the little things that count. These daily acts are the ingredients to my menudo. They're the flavor and spices that make my life exquisite. Although I struggle to maintain this balance, I am reminded of the sacrifice they too have made on my behalf, both directly and indirectly. My husband, my family, and friends keep me grounded as to why I continue the work that I do.

"Keep Calm and Finish your Dissertation"

That's the meme displayed as my cellphone wallpaper. It's a constant reminder of the task that lies ahead and a reflection of my journey thus far. As I previously mentioned, my first semester was a challenge. Not only did I lack a sense of belonging, but I also yearned for an opportunity to engage in more research. Such opportunity came through an announcement for a graduate assistant position with a faculty member in our department. After meeting with Dr. Luke Wood, I knew that I had found my outlet for research! I agreed to a flexible 20-hour per week workload on top of my full-time job and full-time enrollment. After a few weeks of working with Dr. Wood, he asked, "So, what do you wanna do after you graduate?" I hated being asked that question, mainly because I wasn't sure. After giving him a roundabout answer about wanting to work at a community college, he said, "I think you should be a faculty member." Although I had loosely considered this career path a few years prior, I told Dr. Wood that I was keeping my options open, to which he responded, "Well, you still have some time to think about it, but my goal is to prepare you to become a faculty member." His bold statement made me laugh, as I thought, "Okay, sure," not giving it much thought. Soon enough, Dr. Wood took me under his wing and slowly began molding my confidence as a scholar. By the end of my first year, I had presented at a national conference, published my first article, and became managing editor for his journal, the Journal of African American Males in Education (JAAME). By my second year, I became more convinced that the role of a faculty member was one that I was capable of achieving. As I reflect on my journey and growth throughout these three years, I am again reminded of another significant ingredient to my symbolic menudo: mentorship. Such mentorship has come not only from my advisors, Drs. Wood, Gonzalez, and Frank Harris III, but also from my brother and sister scholars. Again, it's the little things that count, whether it be words of encouragement, a brief text to say hello, lunch invitations, introductions to celebrity scholars, or folded notes after each presentation that say "Fantastic work!" or "You killed it!" Their academic, professional, and personal support continues to inspire me to become an advocate for social change, a confident researcher, and a humble servant to our communities.

'Me' time

Aside from balancing my family, work, and school, I've also come to recognize the importance of maintaining my physical and emotional wellbeing during this process. As a thirty-year old woman, my metabolism isn't quite what it used to be. Thus, finding time to exercise has become an important part of my weekly routine. Although I don't mind going alone, having a gym buddy makes the effort a bit more doable. Thankfully, I found a classmate who shares a similar interest and joins me in our quest to stay fit. Aside from its physical health benefits, working out has become a great way to mentally unwind from work, school, and personal stress. However, just as everything else, finding time for the gym has been a challenge. Thus, we typically go at night (around 10 pm) or on the weekends. As an added push to maintain our gym routine, we've made bets on who could lose the most weight by the end of each semester! Although we usually end up calling a truce around finals time, the camaraderie that we've developed as a result of our gym sessions is something for which I am greatly appreciative.

While going to the gym has been a productive outlet for managing my stress, I find it necessary to also indulge in a little "me time." Living in sunny San Diego, I'm fortunate to have many options, including going to the beach, going on a hike, hanging out at a café, watching the sunset, or just chillin' at a park. However, my favorite "me time" consists of taking my family's dog, Princess, to the beach. Rather than bringing my books or laptop, I simply pack a small blanket, some snacks, and a pillow. After letting Princess enjoy her initial sprint to the ocean and her usual seagull chase up and down the sand, we trot our way back to our blanket and soak up the warm sun. The cool ocean breeze and the calming sound of the waves produce a personalized relaxation soundtrack. These moments allow me to re-center my spirit and reflect on why I chose to follow this path in academia. As a Latina, I feel obligated to accomplish my goals, not only for myself, but also for my *familia*, my community, and my profession.

Maintaining a Well-Balanced Diet

As with many Latinos, food always has a way of bringing my *familia* together. Chef *Papi* (aka, my Pops) is well known by both family and friends for his culinary skills. While his recipes for *chile con carne*, *caldo de pollo*, and *ceviche* are to die for, it's his passion and technique that never cease to amaze me. "It's all about presentation." He utters these words each time he prepares a family meal. I watch him take each food item and carefully place them on a platter. He then garnishes the food with colorful spices and finalizes his creation with an enthusiastic *voilà!* While most folks only see (and eat) the finished product, I've been fortunate to witness and partake in the process of his dishes, including *menudo*. Such process isn't simple; it's time consuming, arduous, exhausting, and depending on the dish, can be emotionally and physically draining. As a Latina doctoral student, I've experienced my share of similar sentiments throughout my academic journey. Yet, despite these challenges, the ingredients in my life (*familia*, mentorship, friendship, intellectual and social outlets, encouragement, a sense of belonging, humility, and confidence) have allowed me to maintain a well-balanced path to becoming a critical and socially conscious scholar. And while I can't guarantee that the ingredients to my *menudo* are to your liking, I encourage you, dear reader, to prepare your own recipe for success.

REFERENCES

Marín, G., & Marín, B. V. (1991). *Research with Hispanic populations*. Newbury Park, CA: Sage.

Ojeda, L., Navarro, R. L., & Morales, A. (2011). The role of la familia on Mexican American men's college persistent intentions. *Psychology of Men & Masculinity, 12*(3), 216–229.

Suarez-Orozco, C., & Suarez-Orozco, M. M. (1995). *Transformations: Immigration, family life, and achievement motivation among Latino adolescents*. Stanford, CA: Stanford University Press.

Valenzuela, A. (1999). *Subtractive schooling: U.S. Mexican youth and the politics of caring*. Albany, NY: State University of New York Press.

CHAPTER 21

DEADLINES AND TRYING TO SURVIVE

My Life as a Doctoral Student

James Vines

THE TRANSITION

Prior to enrolling in my PhD program, I was unaware of the changes I would face. As a doctoral student it is important to learn to adjust to the stress, and the countless hours that go into obtaining a PhD. During the PhD process I continue to work to balance and maintain my health and sanity.

Attending classes and completing doctoral coursework is not an issue. I am used to being a student, thus reading and writing papers is something I am used to. Although, life as a student is easy, I would have to learn to adjust to the setting of my institution. As an African American, and native Washingtonian, it is quite a change to attend an institution in a small southern town. I have to realize that I am an outsider both in terms of race, and as a non-southerner. Being the new face in town, people in the community tend to stare, and constantly ask me where I am from. It is a constant reminder that I am not from around here and they know it.

Beyond the Pride and the Privilege: The Stories of Doctoral Students and Work-Life Balance, pages 139–144.

Part-Time Student Status

At the start of my PhD program I was a part-time student. Being a part-time student hindered my ability to connect with my peers in the program. Working during the day and weekends did not leave much room to participate in social activities. My time was divided between my part-time job at a restaurant, working on school assignments, and trying to relax. During my first semester it was difficult to meet other students since all of my courses were online. While sitting at my computer for class, I listened to students and had no idea who they were.

As a part-time student, I began to feel very isolated and disconnected from the other students who had assistantships, and worked within the academic department. Students with an assistantship had more one-on-one contact with faculty members. In addition, they were involved in research projects, and had offices in the academic department. The students with an assistantship seemed to have no problem making friends because they saw each other every day.

Although I was not working in the academic department, my second semester was a little bit easier. I began taking classes on campus which allowed me to interact with more students. While interacting in class, I could finally put a face to the voices and names I would hear from my online course.

MOVIN' ON UP: LIFE AS A GRADUATE ASSISTANT

After my first year in the program, I was offered a graduate research assistantship. As a graduate assistant I find myself having more responsibilities. The change from part-time to full-time student with an assistantship means more responsibilities. In addition, it means a learning experience that is valuable in the academic world.

As a full-time student with a graduate assistantship I have more commitments, and more is expected of me. Despite the high expectations, my life as a graduate assistant is very rewarding. The assistantship afforded me the opportunity to work with faculty members, which is indispensable. As a graduate assistant I have more access to other PhD students. It was so weird; I met more new students in a week than I did the entire first year I was at the institution. Getting to meet other students helped me feel more at ease. I did not feel as isolated as I did my first year. Working in the academic department helped me feel a part of the community. My assistantship gave me the opportunity to write conference proposals, contribute to research projects, and work closely with the librarians at my institution.

As a graduate research assistant, I read, research, write, and think in new ways. In addition, the one-on-one meetings with my supervisor allowed me the chance to receive valuable insight that would be hard to get from a classroom setting. The assistantship is not just a job; it is a peek into the real life of a faculty member, and working in higher education. The research projects afforded me the opportunity to attend academic conferences. During these conferences I interact with other graduate students, and scholars in the education field. The opportunity to attend a conference means I can engage in intellectual dialogue, and realize there is a whole world of people like myself. Later, I realized how vital it is to keep in contact with both faculty and students from these conferences.

Conferences: Not Just a Mini Vacation

Attending academic conferences are necessary because you get to listen to the new research in the field. In addition, networking is a big aspect to conferences. You need to be able to trade contact information with faculty and students from other institutions who share your research interest. Finding someone who shares your research interest could possible lead to co-authoring a publication together. In addition, you never know what job prospects you may find out about through word of mouth. Networking with other students is crucial as these will be your future colleagues once you a complete your degree.

Above all, attending conferences gives me the opportunity as a graduate student to prepare for life as a professor. As a professor you have to balance your teaching, with conference presentations, research, and publications. I have to learn how to balance these demands in order to become a productive faculty member. An individual, who can properly balance their time, is not only productive but successful. As a graduate student in order to remain productive, I am very protective of my time.

Time Can Be on Your Side

The first thing on my agenda every morning is to finish any projects given to me by my supervisor. Once those projects are complete, the next step is to respond to e-mails. In the beginning of my PhD program, I was an e-mail junkie! I felt like I had to constantly check it and respond to everything right away. The constant e-mail checking led me to be less productive. Due to this revelation, I devised a plan to check e-mail during a certain time of day. For me, the best time to respond to e-mails was in the afternoon. Checking e-mails in the afternoon served as a break from my assistantship work. In addition, it allowed me the opportunity to check my mail before starting my evening classes.

Setting Limits

As a PhD student, my first priority is my school work. If I do not succeed academically, I cannot keep my assistantship. In order to ensure success, I set limits and devote proper time for studying and writing. My limits include knowing that at the end of the day, it is time to stop work related to my assistantship. At the end of the day, I bring my assistantship work to a close, or at least a stopping point to pick it up the next day. For me, the end of the day is 5pm. It is necessary to end by 5, in order to prepare for class at 6:00 p.m. In an effort to adhere to limits, I always remember the importance of giving equal amount of time to all of the tasks.

It would be unwise to devote 80% of my time to my assistantship work, but only give 10% to proposal writing, and another 10% to my school work.

Preparation and Deadlines

It is true that time can be on your side, but it is all about preparation. I find it helpful to outline my calendar at the start of each semester. In fact, I keep a copy of my calendar at home, in the office, and one that stays in my book bag at all times. The reason for this is that no matter where I am I can always look to see what upcoming projects I have due. If I plan ahead, I can take sufficient time to work on all assignments, especially class papers. Knowing the due dates for all papers, and proposal deadlines allows me to use my time wisely. The PhD program is a constant reminder that planning and preparation goes a long way. The thing I realize is that no matter what, the work always gets done because I finish everything I start. I have to learn how to live my life around the deadlines and all the work and not make my life all about the deadlines and the work.

Did You Write Today?

Although planning ahead is important, one piece of advice for all graduate students is to write. Writing each day is pivotal, and yes I delete a good portion of what I write, but I am still left with something useful. In the event I only end up with one paragraph, that is one paragraph more I did not have the previous day. Writing each day helps me feel less stressed, and more prepared when those deadlines approach. A lower stress level gives me more energy to engage in activities to promote my personal well-being.

Taking Care of Myself

Personal care is vital to my survival in the PhD program. It may sound trite, but if I do not take care of myself, I am fighting a losing battle. I go out for an hour walk after class, or go to the gym, and make sure to get enough rest at night. Times when I decide to stay up until 2:00 a.m. studying or working on papers means I will not be in the office at 9:00 a.m. the next morning. Also, in order to maintain a healthy diet, I pack my own lunch. My body needs to be properly fueled if I expect it to work well. Also, there are days when I reward myself, and say after class I am going home to watch a movie, or relax and not put in any more office time. Balancing my academic and personal schedule is something that I continue to work on through my doctoral experience. However, in order to maintain a balance in my personal life, I rely on the help of those who love and support me.

The Need for Support

In regards to unconditional support, I turn to my family. I know that no matter what time it is, or what is the issue, home is only a phone call away. My family motivates me when times get hard. While going through the PhD process, it is important to rely on the values, and principles that my family instilled in me when I was younger. I was taught the value of hard work, dedication, and persistence. For me, I am unsure how far I would go in this process without my family always being my biggest supporters.

Another big part of my support comes from other students in my cohort. My cohort is influential as we all go through the PhD journey. We all support each other, organize study groups, and engage in social activities together. In our cohort one thing we do to balance our lives is to meet up in the library early on Saturdays to work and write. Saturday evening is devoted to seeing a movie, dining out, or both. In order to keep our sanity, we have to realize that we are individuals who need to have a social outlet.

Getting Involved

I always enjoy being involved in other activities. When I have the time, I attend meetings of student organizations that are of interest to me. Campus organizations play a major role in maintaining balance. A campus organization gets me out of the office, and allows me to meet other students and build connections.

In fact, I found the dance organization, and membership is open to any student at the university. Although I cannot attend each dance session, I try to attend at least once or twice a week. The dance organization is a healthy way for me to live my life around all of my deadlines. Days when I did not have an evening class, I would enjoy a dance club meeting. Dancing is an excellent way to relieve stress, put the deadlines to the side for a while and have fun. As a doctoral student, it is vital to find a way to incorporate the things I enjoy into my life.

The best way to balance my life around deadlines is to remember that I am more than a doctoral student. I had to remember my hobbies, my likes and dislikes, and activities which made me feel happy. The important thing for me was to not get too consumed into academic life and forget about myself on a holistic level. I did not involve myself in only one activity; I find ways to be involved in the community as well.

Enriching the Community

Through an internet search, I found a local community center where I volunteer. Growing up, I had an appreciation for giving back to the community. At an early age, it was instilled in me to help others, and give my time and energy in order to enrich the area I live in. Community service allows me the opportunity to put academic life to the side and focus on an activity where I am not concerned with school projects or assistantship work.

Finally, I reached out to local members of my fraternity. My involvement with my fraternity allows me the opportunity engage in service projects for the community and for children. My fraternity brothers also serve as an additional support network. One thing that I look forward to is chairing the scholarship committee. The scholarship committee is very dear to me because the money goes towards helping young men obtain a college degree.

A Reflection and Final Thoughts

I would advocate to all PhD students to realize the work is demanding, challenging, but well worth it. The PhD process is not a sprint to finish the dissertation. It is a marathon that challenges your persistence, dedication, and willingness to push past all obstacles. It is up to me to find my voice, to remember there will always be deadlines, but I also have a life to live.

As I reflect on my doctoral journey I would have to say in relation to work life balance one of the important things to remember is to enjoy the process and have fun. The doctoral journey can be intellectually taxing, but it is truly a unique experience that is unlike any other academic degree. I have found that time flies by, and if I do not take time out to enjoy it I will miss out on a lot. Interacting with my cohort gives me the opportunity to get to know them on a personal level. My cohort is like a mini family, and our academic department is like my home away from home. We help encourage and support one another. I keep in mind that I do not have to go through this process alone. My positive experience in the doctoral program has helped me serve as a resource and role model for new students. I find as I continue to maintain a healthy work-life balance, that offering support and guidance to the new cohort is a way to give back to the program that has given so much to me.

NOTES

Chapter 10

1. Green, A. L., & Scott, L. V. (Eds.). (2003). Journey to the Ph.D.: How to navigate the process as African Americans. Sterling, VA: Stylus.

Chapter 11

1. I would like to thank Ildikó Balogh, Olga Bársony, Adrienn Fekete, Orsolya Szabó and László Zsigó for their invaluable comments on an earlier draft of this chapter. I also appreciate the comments and suggestions offered by the reviewers of an earlier version.

Chapter 14

1. I love you.
2. You're crazy.

Chapter 20

1. *Si se Puede* is the motto of the United Farm Workers, which serves as a guiding principle that has served to inspire confidence, courage, and risk-taking.

Beyond the Pride and the Privilege: The Stories of Doctoral Students and Work-Life Balance, pages 145–146.

2. Menudo is a traditional Mexican soup typically served at breakfast. This past New Years day, my father taught me how to make this specialty dish. After 6.5 hours of intense preparation, my menudo was ready! Upon reflection, I realized that this arduous process was symbolic of my path towards completing my degree. Although incredibly time consuming, the end result is worth every minute!
3. The Puente Project is an academic preparation program whose mission is to increase the number of educationally underrepresented students who enroll in four-year colleges and universities, earn degrees, and return to their communities as leaders and mentors to future generations.

AUTHOR BIOGRAPHIES

Paul Artale is a doctoral student in the Adult, Higher, and Lifelong Education (HALE) program at Michigan State University. His research focuses on how work life initiatives improve employee performance and benefit the organization as a whole. Paul is very grateful to the College of Education at MSU for their encouragement and sponsorship of his research. Paul currently works as Director of Student Leadership Programs and Campus Activities at the University of Michigan-Flint. Paul is Italian-Canadian, 35 years old, and is a huge fan of the original Karate Kid movies and wrestling from the 1980s. His family consists of his wife Sherri and his son Alessio. A former defensive lineman at the University of Toronto and college football coach, Paul now spends spare his time speaking to audience's about work life balance, overcoming challenges, and improving their speaking skills. More about Paul can be found by visiting www.paulartale.com

Charlotte Achieng-Evensen is a third year Kenyan American doctoral student in Education at Chapman University. She completed her MA in Education where her research focused on teaching writing to high school students. Professionally, she has taught in the K– 12 system for the past sixteen years, spending eight of those years as an educator in Papua New Guinea. Her most recent classroom includes teaching literature and coordinating a university preparatory program in the Los

Beyond the Pride and the Privilege: The Stories of Doctoral Students and Work-Life Balance, pages 147–153.

Angeles area. Currently, she serves her school district as a Teacher Specialist. Her research interests lie in Indigenous Philosophies and research methodologies, as well as, professional development for teacher practice. She can be contacted at: evens102@mail.chapman.edu.

David M. Brown is a doctoral candidate in the University of Kentucky's Department of Educational Policy Studies and Evaluation. Under the guidance of Dr. John Thelin, his research focuses on the history of higher education, with emphases on student life and student cultures. His other scholarly interests include honors programs and the strategies that colleges and universities use to market themselves. He holds a graduate certificate in College Teaching and Learning from the University of Kentucky and was nominated for that institution's Outstanding Teaching Award for teaching assistants in 2014. In his spare time, David enjoys travelling and being outdoors; he and his wife are closing in on their goal of camping in each of the 50 states.

Melissa Rae Byrne, MEd is Assistant Director of Curriculum for St. Charles Community Unit School District in St. Charles, Illinois. Currently she is a doctoral candidate at Aurora University and expects to complete her degree in early 2015. Her research agenda explores the influence and impact that philosophical perspectives have on educators' understanding and implementation of curriculum and pedagogy. In 2011, she was one of nine finalists for Illinois Teacher of the Year and earned an award of excellence in teaching. Melissa is very involved in the community and is a volunteer co-director for the Greater Fox River Valley Chapter of Operation Snowball, a drug and alcohol prevention and leadership group for high school students and also serves on the Board of Directors for Operation Snowball, Inc.

Keith Alan Cunningham lives, works, and goofs around in the Central Texas college town of San Marcos with his wife and two young ones. He works for the local ISD in the Social Studies Department. His PhD is in Education with a focus on School Improvement from Texas State University. He is currently 42 years old; demographically he is largely a mongrel, with significant doses of Celt and German in the not too distant genealogical past. When not playing around with his family, he spends as much time as possible reading, swimming, biking, and gardening; finally graduating has made such pastimes much more feasible.

Taurean Davis is an African American doctoral student at Clemson University in the Educational Leadership (EDL) program and works as a doctoral research and teaching assistant. He received his MEd in Counselor Education/Student Affairs from Clemson and has worked in higher education for over five years. Additionally, he has mentored, supervised, and taught graduate students throughout his professional and academic career and currently teaches students within Clemson's masters program in Student Affairs. Currently, at 32, he is writing his dissertation focusing on digital media interventions for EDL faculty to help integrate digital media and collaborative learning into the EDL curriculum. His other research interests include: digital media literacy among college students, web-based learning environments, technology as access to education, and social media usage in student affairs. He is originally from Duncan, SC.

Chinasa A. Elue, PhD is an assistant professor at Kent State University in the Educational Administration program. Her ongoing research uses phenomenological methods to explore perceptions of increased debt on the college choice and enrollment of rural, low-income students. Prior to working at Kent State, Dr. Elue served as a Research Associate with the University Council of Education Administration (UCEA) Center for Law in Leadership and Education. Her ongoing research agenda focuses on issues of access and equity for underserved students, law and policy in education, and financial aid policy.

Dr. B. Genise Henry works internationally to support the strengthening of relationships across cultures through a foreign exchange student program and nationally with school districts and educational organizations to support school improvement initiatives as an educational consultant. In addition to her global ethics work, she serves in the capacity of a State Literacy Liaison at the Institute for Public School Initiatives at the University of Texas at Austin where she supports school districts that have received the Texas Literacy Initiative grant. Dr. Henry graduated with her PhD in School Improvement at Texas State University-San Marcos where she was named a David L. Clark Scholar and featured in the Texas Monthly Magazine as a Barbara Jackson Scholar. Her dissertation research focused on spirituality in the experiences of African American female doctoral students, where she used qualitative methods that incorporated participatory research with ethnography and social cartography. Dr. Henry is a wife and a mother of two children with whom she credits their love and support for her ability to be successful in all that she does away from home.

Olga Martinez Hickman is a Senior Field Trainer for the University of Texas at Austin. Her work promotes school improvement and success in the area of language and literacy. She has numerous years of experience that include supporting literacy initiatives across the state of Texas. Her background includes knowledge in leadership, literacy, and second language acquisition for diverse learners. She holds two Master of Arts degrees, one in Reading and one in Educational Leadership. She is currently a doctoral student at the University of Texas at Arlington, with a focus on communities of color, which will support her aim to ensure that all students receive a fair and equitable high quality education.

Jennifer Horace is doctoral candidate in the Educational Leadership program at Clemson University. She is an African American female born and raised in Chicago, Illinois, and is a graduate of University of Illinois, Urbana-Champaign and

Indiana University. Currently she works at Purdue University in the Office of the Dean of Students and Office of Institutional Equity.

Éva Kardos is Junior Lecturer in Linguistics at the University of Debrecen in Hungary. She teaches academic writing, descriptive grammar, and semantics at the undergraduate level. She is also interested in the teaching and testing of English as a second language. As a graduate student, she conducted research at Indiana University and the University of Texas at Austin. At Texas, she was a Fulbright visiting student researcher. She completed her PhD in Linguistics at the University of Debrecen in 2012. Outside of academia, she loves to travel and discover new cultures. Although she has high aspirations in her career, family is most important to her.

Daniel and **Kaiwipuni Lipe** both earned their doctoral degrees from the College of Education at the University of Hawai'i at Mānoa (UHM). Daniel (Westernband Cherokee) grew up in the woods and along the rivers of Oregon. His dissertation focused on indigenous knowledge systems and western science. He is currently an educational specialist who supports underrepresented students to complete their college degrees in STEM fields. Kaiwipuni (Native Hawaiian) was raised on O'ahu and is a 2013–2014 Mellon Hawai'i doctoral fellow. Her dissertation focused on transforming higher education institutions into indigenous places of learning. Together they have a son and daughter.

Bibiana Mancera was born and raised in El Paso, Texas. She is of Mexican descent and the oldest of three. Bibiana is married to Ray and has to children, Marcos (11) and Isabella (4). She is the first in her family to receive a Bachelor's Degree (1996) and a Master's (2006), both from the University of Texas at El Paso (UTEP). She is currently working on her PhD in Interdisciplinary Health Sciences and plans to complete her dissertation by December of 2015. Bibiana has over 14 years of experience within the University of Texas System, 11 or them with UTEP. She has been the Project Manager for the Hispanic Health Disparities Research Center (HHDRC), a National Institutes of Health Disparities P20 Center of Excellence at UTEP for five years, where she oversees the day to day programmatic operations of the Center. Bibiana became interested in research while at the HHDRC and is currently involved in the VIDA II (Violence, Intimate Relationships, and Drugs among Latinas/os), (PI, Provencio-Vasquez), (NIH), Phase II of the study, conducting focus groups with women and men regarding intimate partner violence, substance abuse, and high risk sexual behavior.

Edna Martinez, PhD is an assistant professor of Educational Leadership at California State University, San Bernardino. Her research interests are centered on two strands of interrelated inquiry. In the first line of inquiry, she explores organizational change within community colleges that have adopted baccalaureate degree programs. Drawing from the first strand, in the second, she seeks to understand how modifications to existing policies and practices shape educational experiences and opportunities for traditionally underserved/underrepresented students.

Marlen Kanagui-Muñoz is a postdoctoral resident at Kaiser Permanente, Richmond. She recently completed her doctorate from the University of Missouri in Counseling Psychology with a minor in Multicultural Psychology. She has published and presented in the area of Latina/o psychology focusing on cultural influences on coping and strength-based approaches in measurement. In her free time, Marlen enjoys spending time with her family, cooking, and taking on do-it-yourself projects.

José Muñoz is a Gus T. Ridgel Fellow and doctoral candidate in Educational Leadership and Policy Analysis at the University of Missouri. His research focuses on higher education finance and financial aid and their impact on racial/ethnic minority students. Outside of his professional interests, José enjoys golfing, fishing, and playing music with his family.

Agustina Veny Purnamasari is a doctoral student at School of Education, Iowa State University, Ames, Iowa and a Fulbright fellow. Her research interests range from organization and administration; human resources issues at higher education institution; university department chairs; to Catholic education. More about Agustina research, publications, current, and past activities can be found at http://agustinavp.wix.com/agustinavp

Dagoberto Eli Ramirez earned his Doctor of Education Degree in Educational Leadership from the University of Texas-Pan American in Edinburg, Texas in May 2013. Dagoberto: was born in Roma, Texas on October 8, 1956; graduated from Roma High School in May 1975; attended the University of Oklahoma from September 1975 to May 1979; traveled to Mexico City and taught English to adults from August 1979 to May 1980; returned to Texas and taught at Ringgold Junior High School in Rio Grande City CISD from 1982 to 1985; attended Pan American University, completing his Bachelor's Degree in English and History in 1985; taught English, History, Geography, and Leadership at La Joya ISD between August 1985 and 1998; worked as an Education Specialist at Region One ESC in Edinburg, Texas from 1998 to 2001; attended the University of Texas-Pan American between June 2000 and December 2002 earning his Master's degree in Educational Leadership; was La Joya ISD Social Studies Coordinator from 2001 to 2012; and, is currently the Resource Development Coordinator at the 501(c)(3) non-profit Edinburg Housing Authority writing grants and securing other resources focused on improving the educational lives of children of low-income families living in the authority's five housing developments.

Juhanna Rogers is a doctoral candidate at Indiana University. Juhanna is a native of Newark, New Jersey and a Penn State University – Atloona alumni. At the age of 32, she is the founding director of an international study abroad experience, a research associate for Great Lakes Equity Center, and adjunct faculty for Africana Studies at Indiana University Purdue University Indianapolis. In addition to her doctoral work, she is a co-parent and artist. Her son, Nile, is 9 years old and inspires her artistic and academic work. She would like to dedicate this chapter to her mother, grandmothers, aunties, and my secret Life of PhDs who challenged me and believed in me. Thank you to my son's dad, Eugene, for doing more than your share so that I can live my dreams. To my dad, brother, and Poppa Nathan for teaching me to push myself harder every day. I am because of you all.

Leslie Jo (LJ) Shelton is a higher education/student affairs scholar focused on exploring the learning and development of students in higher education. She earned her PhD in Higher, Adult, and Lifelong Education from Michigan State University in May 2014. In her dissertation, LJ examined the experiences of undocumented Latino/a college students who demonstrate resilience in navigating higher education. Her teaching and scholarship focus on the college experiences and identity development of diverse students, issues of equity for underrepresented students, learning outcomes of education abroad, and the scholarship of teaching and learning. Prior to starting the HALE program at MSU, LJ worked full time as a student affairs educator and graduated from Ohio University with a Masters of Education in College Student Personnel. She also earned a Bachelor's of Science in Sociology/Criminology and a Women's Studies certificate from Ohio University. Go Bobcats! LJ identifies as a life-long learner, traveler, tea drinker, yoga enthusiast, and runner.

Marissa Vasquez Urias earned her EdD in Educational Leadership from San Diego State University. Her scholarly work addresses factors impacting the success (e.g., persistence, achievement, attainment, transfer, labor market outcomes) of male students of color, particularly Latino and African American men, in the community college. As a former transfer student, Marissa understands firsthand the challenges faced by community college students and is committed to being an agent of change for education and social justice.

In addition to this work, Marissa has been engaged in research-to-practice initiatives designed to use data to increase student success in both K– 12 and higher education, at the national, state, and local levels. As a consultant for the national initiative, "Achieving the Dream", Marissa worked at various community colleges, guiding faculty, staff, and administrators through a process of data collection to identify gaps in student achievement, as well as implementing and improving strategies for institutional effectiveness. Marissa earned her MA in Counseling with a specialization in College Counseling and Student Development from the University of San Diego and her BA in English from the University of California, Berkeley.

James E. Vines is a PhD candidate in Educational Leadership, Higher Education, program at Clemson University. As part of his PhD studies he has completed the Policy Studies Certificate from the Strom Thurmond Institute of Government and Public Affairs at Clemson University. Prior to his doctoral work, Mr. Vines was a Mental Health Counselor in Washington, DC and a Graduate Hall Director at Virginia State University. Currently, Mr. Vines is working on his dissertation titled "An Explanatory Embedded Case Study of the Proposed Megan Meier Cyberbullying Prevention & Tyler Clementi Higher Education Anti-Harassment Statutes". His ongoing research agenda covers cyberbullying and the creation of federal and state statutes.

CPSIA information can be obtained at www.ICGtesting.com
Printed in the USA
BVOW09s1522071214

378012BV00006B/19/P

9 781623 969066